Items should be returned on or before the last date
shown below. Items not already requested by other
borrowers may be renewed in person, in writing or by
telephone. To renew, please quote the number on the
barcode label. To renew online a PIN is required.
This can be requested at your local library.
Renew online @ **www.dublincitypubliclibraries.ie**
Fines charged for overdue items will include postage
incurred in recovery. Damage to or loss of items will
be charged to the borrower.

Leabharlanna Poiblí Chathair Bhaile Átha Cliath
Dublin City Public Libraries

Baile Átha Cliath
Dublin City

Walkinstown Library
Tel. 4558159

Date Due	Date Due	Date Due
18 NOV 2014		

The New Dubliners

Daniel Zuchowski

Literary Publishing

Dublin 2014

Published by Literary Publishing in Dublin in 2014

www.literarypublishinghouse.com

The names and some of the details in this book have been changed to protect the identity of individuals.

Second edition

ISBN 978-0-9928132-1-5

Cover illustration

Liffey Walk © Paula Pohli

www.thenewdubliners.com

CONTENTS

NOT NOW

Bye-bye, bitch, bye-bye!!! Woahh! *You don't know a goddamn thing about the real world... Ehh... Here's a short sharp lesson...* What the fuuuuuck?! Must've left it on repeat. Still fuckin' buzzing. Did I sleep? How long? Where's my phone? Oh, she's not sleeping.

"Sorry, I'll turn it off now," I say.

Boxers on my pale ass. Dizzy. And it's off.

"Sorry about that..." I apologise in my morning baritone. "Were you able to get any sleep with that thing blasting?"

"Yeah, no problem," she says like there was really no problem.

And she somehow manages to look fresh and rested, lying on the side, smiling. Her long black hair all tousled. Most of it behind her, on the pillow.

"Was that heavy metal?" she asks when I come back from the bathroom after a quick shower and a thorough mouth wash.

"Yeah, I suppose you can call it heavy metal, but these guys, the band, call it rock'n'roll."

"The lyrics are funny," she says.

"Are they?"

"Yeah, I listened to them."

"Did you? So you didn't sleep then!"

"I did."

"They're called Motorhead," I say, and that makes her laugh. She clearly hasn't heard of Motorhead before. She might have lived in a bubble until now.

"It's slang for *speed* – the drug," I explain, because I don't want her to laugh at one of my favourite bands.

"Is it? Really?"

"Yeah, they used to take loads of that stuff. And who knows, maybe they still do."

"Ah, OK."

"Did you have a good time at the party?" I ask.

"Yeah. It was fun. And good food, too, wasn't it?"

I'm just after washing my teeth scrupulously, but I can still feel the pungent anchovy paste and the cheesy garlic dip in my mouth (on the tongue maybe? I forgot to scrub the tongue!), so I only grunt. And I burp quietly.

"Do you remember how I splashed the wine all over the wall?!" I change the topic.

"Yes!" she giggles. "How did you do that?!"

"Don't know. Was trying to uncork the bottle, stupidly holding it up in the air instead of putting it on the table, or on the floor, and when I finally pulled the cork out, the wine just splashed all over the wall! And on Marco's jumper!" I laugh, but I'm slightly embarrassed. "He had to change it. Must've been pissed off…"

"No, he wasn't," she laughs too.

I can't see her smile, because I'm lying with my right ear on her navel, but I can remember it very vividly – it's beautiful.

"I'm sure he was. At one point the whole party was pure chaos…" I chortle.

"No, he wasn't. Don't worry."

"Hey," I say after a moment of reflection, "but you were there in the kitchen at that point! We were talking about rugby…"

"Yeah?"

"You said you'll support the Irish team. It was us two against the other guys who'd support The All Blacks."

"Yeah."

"I'll ask Paco to talk to Marco and check how much he paid for the jumper. I'll give him the money for it. When I splashed the wine all over him, he said it was a brand new jumper!"

Laughing loud, I swap my ears on her belly. She fondles with my hair. It feels nice.

"Do you remember how we rode the bike through the night?" I chuckle. "It was crazy! People staring at us and laughing. Shaking their heads. They were sure we'd slip on the snow and crash into one of the taxis. And me too I thought we would."

"Yeah, but did you really last ride a bike ten years ago?" she asks amazed.

"Why?"

"Cos you told me so when we were on the bike."

"Yeah! Err…" I scratch my head. "No, it actually wasn't ten years ago. I was in Phoenix Park last year chasing the deer."

It makes her laugh, which in turn makes my head bounce on her flat belly.

"Oh…." I continue, "and I went to a grocer's on a bike when I was in my parents' summer house last year. Or it might've been two years ago. But don't get me wrong, I like the whole idea of cycling, y'know? But the truth is I prefer walking. Since I went to university, I've always lived in the city centre, close to everything, y'know? So there was no need."

"And for fun you never did?" she asks.

"Yeah, last night!" we both burst out laughing.

***

Last night, at around half past one, Marco and Paco started kicking their guests out – the last few heads that were still there. Paco whispered into Oskar's ear that it was time to go home.

"What d'you mean?!" Oskar was surprised. "I'm waiting here for you! Aren't we going to O'Reilly's?!"

"No, not tonight, man! Some other time," Paco mumbled.

"But you kept asking me all night to go there with you after the party."

"Yeah, but I'm too drunk now, man."

Paco had wanted to check out the rock nights they have in O'Reilly's at weekends, and Oskar had said he would join him, but, according to the Spanish girl that Oskar is now in bed with, Paco then got really locked. He apparently puked over the balcony railing. A few times he did.

When Oskar found his way out of the filthy – at least under Paco's balcony – apartment block, he spotted one of the girls from the party. It was that Spanish girl in a bright green flower-power dress that he had spent loads of time talking to about music, rugby and Irish giants. She was unlocking her bike, but it was very cold – as cold as it can get at the beginning of January in Ireland, or even colder – so he asked her if she was sure she was going to cycle. And when she said she was, he enquired where to.

They happened to be going in the same direction, so she offered Oskar a ride. But standing on the snow- and ice-covered footpath, shaking in his light oxfords, Oskar thought she was mad (Mind you, that particular winter was a total disaster in Ireland: loads of snow, no public transport, the airport shut down, water pipes frozen, and no food left in shops. No, actually there was food, but they ran out of road salt.). So, as soon as he had established that, he knew he wanted to go with her. But he only agreed on one condition: he wanted to pedal.

Though pedalling wasn't easy in the winter coat that Oskar had on, the strong wind coming in from the Irish sea nicely pushed the bike away from Ringsend towards Dublin 8, where they were heading.

She sat sideways on the crossbar, looking rather relaxed, her hands wrapped in a pair of brightly coloured knitted mittens, holding the handlebar stem firmly.

On the junction with Lombard Street, beside the rear entrance to Trinity College, Oskar started losing control of the bike, so the Spanish girl demanded to change him. He agreed for the craic, and also because she was quite adamant about it, but sitting between her arms, with his long legs dangling low on one side, riding past drunken crowds scrambling their way home or to another party, and between taxis spinning their wheels in the snow, wasn't that much fun after all. Therefore, as soon as they rode into Dame Street, Oskar offered to swap again. But, as hilarious as it was, cycling both of them up the ice-covered Lord Edward's Street towards Christchurch proved to be too big an effort for him. They had to jump off the bike and walk instead. But instead of walking home, Oskar suggested a drink in The Bull & Castle.

By then, it was almost closing time and the pub was already emptied, but the bartender agreed to serve them a round. Oskar had a double whiskey and coke, she ordered a pint of lager. Properly plastered, they had a nice chat and loads of laughs – so much that the security guy had to approach them twice before they finally got up and left.

When the pub doors had been shut and locked behind them, they pulled on their big winter hats and faced each other to say goodbye. But instead of bidding a farewell, they kissed so passionately that the ice under their feet melted momentarily. And a short moment later, their winter attire was hastily being removed in Oskar's apartment around the corner.

It seemed to Oskar that they'd made love for a long time, and in many different positions, but he didn't remember much of it the next day. Yet he did remember that he hadn't come. And that neither had she. In fact, he had been so hammered that at one point his penis had just flopped out of her as soft as a marshmallow. She managed to resuscitate it with the kiss of life, though, and then quickly and hard jumped on it, rubbing her clitoris at the speed of light, but before they noticed, Oskar had flopped out again. And then they just gave up and passed out – or they passed out without actually giving up.

***

Now she comes back from the bathroom. Still naked. Gorgeous body. Slim, but not skinny. Nicely toned. Must be all the cycling and yoga. Jumps into the bed and cuddles in with her back towards me. Her hair isn't the freshest, though. Reeks of cigarette smoke from last night's party. Must've been smoking on the balcony and that's when she saw him throw up. Great boobs. Rather small, smallish, but very firm. And her hips and bum! Just perfect! Like a juicy watermelon in the middle of a hot summer.

Kiss on the neck and the back. A number of times. Very softly. Seems to enjoy it. Palms of my fingers down her spine. Gently. And up. And down again. Hair swept away from her shoulder to make room for another kiss. My left hand on her left buttock. Caressing gently. I get very aroused. Even more so when she presses her bum against my groin. Then, still with her back towards me, and her neck under my lips, she grips me with her left hand. I goose her. She tightens the grip. My hand moves slowly in-between her thighs, from behind. She's not shaved, but she feels trimmed. And she's very wet. I push my hand further between her thighs and slowly slide the three middle fingers from the top of her pubic mound all the way down. She purrs. I massage her very sensually. But she doesn't want any foreplay. Pulls me hard and slides me in. The first two times very shallowly, but then she throws her hips backwards to make me enter her deeper and harder. Yes, without a condom. We were doing it for two hours last night like that, so what would be the point in using one now?

***

Oskar then asks what her name is. He remembers that the name is rather unusual, and perhaps that's why he can't recall it – that's his excuse anyway. He's pretty sure she won't mind. And he's right – she just laughs and says she knew he wouldn't remember. Then, they cuddle again, but only for a short while, because now Oskar needs to run to work. Yes, on a Saturday, but it's an open day in the place where he works, and the manager has asked him to help her out.

Before Oskar leaves, he takes a quick shower. There's no time for proper breakfast, though. But even if there was, the fridge is empty anyway, save for a bottle of white wine, some gin, three bottles of Lucozade, ketchup and a jar of gherkins. He goes for Lucozade and one of those energy bars stashed in the cupboard above the fridge.

He wants to meet Irune for lunch, but she says she's going to go home and get some sleep. They agree to meet in the evening for dinner and a movie – at his place.

On his way to the office, Oskar's a bit anxious about the fact that he most certainly smells like a distillery, and that after all the sucking, licking and biting his lips are red and swollen like a ripe tomato. But he's extremely happy. He feels he has found a really nice girl. He can't wait to see her again.

At work, when he answers the first set of queries from a prospective customer, he feels his mobile vibrate in the inside pocket of his jacket. He ignores it. But it rings again, so he pops out for a moment to check what's going on. And he's surprised to see Ester's number beaming from his BlackBerry.

Ester is his most recent ex-girlfriend. They only broke up two days ago – just a few days after their New Year's trip to Manchester. She's back at home in the Czech Republic now. She got three weeks off for Christmas from the family she lives with as an au pair. Oskar rings her back.

"Hey! Sorry I missed your call, but I'm at work," he explains.

"Oh! I didn't know. I shouldn't bother you," Ester apologies, but Oskar instantly senses that something is wrong.

"No problem, don't worry. What's up?"

"Did you get my email yesterday?" she asks tentatively.

"Err... No. I haven't checked my private mail for the last two or three days. Why?"

"I wrote that I still didn't get my period," Oskar's heart starts pounding like cannon ball fire. "And that I was thinking about repeating the pregnancy test. And now it's positive!" she starts sobbing. "But I can't be pregnant. It's impossible!" And she breaks down completely.

***

Oskar was shocked. He had entirely forgotten about the whole thing. Actually, he hadn't forgotten, but he had presumed everything was fine. After all, Ester had done a pregnancy test on Christmas Eve and it was negative. And as pregnancy tests are ninety-eight percent accurate, Oskar had never doubted the result.

Ester took that test on Christmas Eve, because the night before they went their separate ways for Christmas holidays, the condom had burst. And they had only found out about it when it was too late.

That had never before happened to any of them, so, with trembling hands and wide-opened eyes, they immediately started researching what should be done in situations like that. They'd heard about the morning-after pill, but Oskar didn't have any in his first aid kit. Nor did Ester.

Oskar ventured into town, hoping to find a pharmacy and get the pill, but at 2 a.m. there were no pharmacies open that he knew of. In the meantime, however, Ester read that the pill would work provided it was taken in less than twenty-four hours after the intercourse, so, when Oskar came back, they decided to stop panicking and wait until the morning.

Oskar's flight was before noon, and Ester's was one day later, but in those circumstances he didn't want to go anywhere. He wanted to postpone the trip and accompany Ester to the GP's. But Ester insisted he went home. She was sure she would be fine.

Before the plane took off, Oskar had received a message from Ester that the doctor had given her a prescription for the pill and explained that if she took the pill immediately, there would only be a tiny chance she could get pregnant. The doctor had also asked her to wait for four days before she performed the pregnancy test.

Both of them were extremely anxious about the whole thing. They had only met two months before, and although they did have a lot of sympathy for each other, there didn't seem to be any deeper feelings involved. Moreover, that petite brunette of curvy figure, with big, green eyes in a face that looked much younger than it really was, had only come to Dublin for a year to improve her English. After that she had been planning to go back home to complete her degree. She had a year left at university. And there was a thesis to be written.

Oskar was very supportive and made sure Ester knew she could rely on him no matter what happened. He even joked that a positive test would be a great Christmas present for his parents, since they had the tendency to joke about him approaching his fourth decade and having not that much time left to start breeding.

But joking aside, they were on tenterhooks for the four days. They had indeed been reassured that the pill would work, but Ester had been exactly midway through her menstrual cycle when it all happened. And being young and healthy, her body was more than ready to conceive. They were not sure at all if they could sleep soundly.

Oskar wanted Ester to stay clear of alcohol until she performed the test, and even though she found it amusing, she acquiesced. But her parents were shocked – someone with such great love for red wine had not touched a drop all night! And it was Christmas! She must have come up with some great excuse to be able to keep her old folks at bay.

***

Ester planned to do the test after dinner on Christmas Eve. And Oskar wanted to be with her while she was doing it. She promised to ring him once she was in the bathroom ready to go.

And what a relief it was for them to find out that the result was negative. With their hands still shaking, they could now rejoin their families at the Christmas tables and finally start enjoying the festivities.

After Christmas, Ester and Oskar went to Prague. They spent three days there. Oskar had never been to the Czech Republic before, but Ester's university was there – though her family lived in a small town outside the capital – so she was eager to show him 'her' Prague.

And she did, dragging them through snow and bitter cold, and then going through gallons of mulled wine and beer in the cosy bars of the Old Town to warm themselves up. And they fucked there like rabbits. Her period was due shortly, so they were happy not to have to be as careful as they had been before.

In Manchester, where they went for New Year's Eve after Prague, she ate like a horse. But it wasn't really so obvious at that time, because she had always loved good food, and she would often outeat Oskar. She had all her usual signs of impending period, and even though it was already overdue, they didn't worry – the doctor had warned them that a delayed period could well be expected after a morning-after pill.

After a few days spent together full-time, Ester and Oskar began growing tired of each other. They would get on each other's nerves all the time – maybe apart from the bed – and the heated debates they had always enjoyed having now started to annoy them. Oskar felt it was time to move on.

From Manchester Ester was flying to Prague for another ten days of holidays with her family before she would return to Ireland, but Oskar was flying directly to Dublin. They said goodbye as if they were saying it for the very last time.

A few days later, Oskar sent Ester an email explaining his feelings and asking what she thought of the whole situation. She replied she wanted to give their relationship a chance, to maybe take a short break and see if they missed each other, but Oskar had already decided – he wanted to end it immediately and definitely. He didn't think a break would change anything.

***

"But how?! The other test was negative!" Oskar tries to make sense out of it.

"Yes, but this one is positive!" Ester repeats and gradually stops crying.

"Have you done just this one test today?"

"Yes, I only had one. But I want to do another one later today. A friend of mine works in Prague, so I'll ask her to get me more. And I'll get it from her when she will come home after work. I don't want to buy here. It's only two pharmacies here, and everybody knows everybody, you know..."

"OK. And how are you feeling?"

"My ovaries are sore and my breasts are swollen," she starts sobbing again.

"Oh, fuck!"

"But I usually feel like that before my period," Ester explains. "But it was never so delayed!"

"Yeah, your period was supposed to be over a week ago... But don't worry now," Oskar tries to calm her down, "just try to do another test as quickly as possible. And please let me know the results immediately. I'll be waiting."

"I will. And I'll do two tests this time. Just to be sure."

***

A text message from Ester to Oskar:

> I did two tests from two different manufacutrers. Both says i'm pregnant.

A text message from Oskar to Ester:

> Can you talk now?

A text message from Ester to Oskar:

> No, my parents are at home now. I'll call you on skype later when they will go to sleep.

A text message from Oskar to Ester:

> OK! I'll have my Skype on. Call me any time.

***

Fuck me! FUUUCK ME!!! That's it! Is it? Is this how it feels like to find out? My heart will fuckin' pop out in a moment. I think I'll get sick. Doubt it if she'll want to keep it. I'd like to. But can we do it together? It wasn't supposed to be like this.

Live together? How? We weren't supposed to hold on to it. Should've finished it earlier. It just lasted far too long. And all that sex without protection. Fuck! She could've actually got pregnant on our first night. No, she had a period after that. Don't want to live with her and a child in some fuckin' shithole. But to have it would be nice. But she won't give it to me like that, will she? I'd be a good father, though. Maybe it would work out for us? At least for the first two or three years...

***

"Hey..." Ester says in that typical soft voice of hers. "The walls here are really thin. I have to be very quiet."

"No problem, I can hear you. How are you feeling?"

"Well... Alright, I guess. I think my parents are starting to suspect something. But I'm trying to behave normally when they are around," she says calmly.

"Yeah, I'm sure they are. First, you didn't want to drink, and now..."

"Uhm... I will go to gynaecologist on Monday to confirm."

"Right, tomorrow's Sunday. Fuck. That's another day of waiting."

"Yeah, I know."

"Is there a gynaecologist in your town?"

"Yes, but I'll go to Prague anyway."

"Right... Do you have enough money?"

"Yes, I do. Thanks." she says and then she pauses for a moment before she adds, "I can't believe it!" And she lets out a sharp snort.

"Yeah..." I snort too. "But let's wait until the doctor confirms. Maybe the tests are fucked up."

"But all of them?!"

"Yeah, I know!" I say, but I do hope they're all fucked up.

"But yeah, let's wait until Monday. I am very tired now."

"I'd like to be with you," I say.

"Yes, I would like to be with you, too. It isn't easy to be here alone."

"Yes, I was thinking about coming over," I say.

"No! Here? With my parents? So suddenly?! Then they would definitely find out."

"Yeah, but if you're really pregnant, we'll need to tell them anyway," I try to think logically.

"Yes, but my plane is next week anyway," she reminds me.

"Are you sure you'll be fine until then?"

"Yes, I think. I try to not think about it," she explains, clearly saddened.

"And how are you feeling?"

"Good. Just tired. I will take a shower when we will finish, and go to bed."

"Yeah, I'm tired myself," I say.

"Did you go out last night?"

"Yeah, I went to a friend's house party. Slept almost nothing."

She laughs quietly and slags me, "No surprise! Typical!"

"Yeah, I guess…" I admit. "But I've been reading about getting pregnant and all that all day today after work."

"Yes, me too."

***

Oskar cancelled the movie night with Irune and put it all down to family issues back at home. He told her he would probably need to go home for a few days to sort things out. He promised to explain everything later. She seemed understanding.

On Monday, the doctor confirmed that Ester was pregnant. But she was already four weeks pregnant, so that also confirmed Oskar's hypothesis that Ester had conceived earlier – which also explained why the morning-after pill had not worked.

Ester admitted it was a strange feeling to see the embryo during the ultrasonography, and Oskar felt it was unfair she had had to go through the examination alone. He also started to worry about the condition of the embryo, remembering well how much booze they both had downed over their Christmas break, as well as before it. He worried it all could affect the child's condition.

Oskar was also concerned about the fact that Ester had taken the morning-after pill when already pregnant. But Ester explained that she had talked to the doctor about it and that the doctor had said the pill wouldn't have any negative effect on the child. That, however, didn't manage to put Oskar's mind at ease.

Then, as hard as it was for him, he told Ester that since she wanted to complete her degree, he was prepared to move to Prague – she would be studying and he would be working to support the child and her.

He can't have been very persuasive, though, because Ester remained sceptical. But she was happy to hear that Oskar was ready to make such sacrifices. She knew he loved Dublin and that he had his life there.

Ester then admitted that she had already thought about everything and that she knew it wouldn't work out. She was afraid they would eventually start hating each other and that she would then be left alone with the child. And it didn't help when Oskar promised she wouldn't.

Ester went on explaining that she had always thought she would only ever get pregnant if she was in love – true love – and only when she felt she wanted to share that love with yet another person. And she had always believed that being pregnant would be an incredible feeling. But there she was now – terrified.

Then, Ester asked Oskar if he loved her. Disregarding the circumstances, Oskar thought he needed to be honest with her, and so he calmly explained that he did feel much closer to her now, much more attached, but he wasn't sure if he could call that love.

"You see? That's why I think it's not a good idea," she concluded.

"So what do you want to do?" Oskar asked with a noticeable lump in his throat.

"I don't know. But I think it's not the right moment to have a baby. We both have different plans. And what would my parents say? They're already mad at me for taking this gap year."

"Eh, stop worrying about your parents! Doesn't matter what they say or think!" Oskar got clearly annoyed.

"Yes, you are right, but I'm still dependent on them financially, so…"

"Don't worry about that either!" Oskar interrupted. "I said I'd take care of everything."

"Thanks, Oskar," she said quietly and appreciatively, "but I still think it's not the right moment."

"So what do you want to do?" Oskar repeated his question bluntly. He couldn't wait, yet at the same time he dreaded, to hear the answer.

"I don't know… but…"

"Are you considering abortion?" Oskar interrupted her again.

"Hmmm… I was thinking about it, yes," she admitted, reluctantly. "What do you think?"

"You know my opinion on abortion in situations like this. We discussed it the other day," Oskar said brusquely.

"Yes, we did. But we were in different situation then. I didn't know how serious were you about it."

"Rather serious."

Oskar knew abortion would be a terrible thing to go through, but he felt desperate. He believed it would be the lesser of two evils, yet he didn't want to admit it – not before himself, not before Ester. He was also ashamed of himself for trying to make Ester take the burden of the decision on her shoulders, and then be forced to carry its stigma.

He did his best, though, to make her understand that no matter what she decided, he would support her unconditionally – and never question.

They then decided to sleep it over and discuss it again in the morning.

But Oskar didn't want to waste any time. Since he knew abortion was illegal in Ireland, he rushed online to see what the procedure was like in Britain. And he was surprised at how accessible and how relatively cheap it was there. They even had discounts for people travelling from Ireland.

The first result that came up in Google search was Marie Stopes – a clinic that had quite a few locations in England, as well as an information centre in Dublin. He sent Ester a link and explained that the website was quite informative. She replied that she had already found it herself and was reading it now, too.

Oskar noticed that this communication with Ester had brought him some relief, and so he again felt ashamed of himself. But somehow he also felt that they were making the right decision. He did worry about Ester, though. She seemed rather calm and restrained, but inside she could be in emotional tatters.

The next morning, Ester and Oskar behaved as if the decision had already been made. They went through the basic options for termination as outlined on the website, which to both of them seemed terrifying, and found contact details for a phone consultation that was available to patients from overseas.

Having better English, Oskar offered to call the clinic to make an appointment, but there they wanted to speak to the patient. Ester had to ring them herself. She did, and she was happy with the advice and help that she had received there.

The clinic in Bristol seemed to be the handiest. Everything would be done there in one day – in around two hours, to be precise.

Before the procedure, Ester would first come to Dublin, and then they would fly over to Bristol together. They also decided, as recommended by the clinic, that after the procedure they would stay in Bristol overnight.

***

Ester arrived in Dublin on an evening flight, and Oskar was at the airport to collect her. She had organised another four days off for herself, making up some family-issues story, in order to be able to stay with Oskar for at least a few days after the procedure.

When they met, they hugged like they had never hugged before. And on the airport bus back to town, Oskar held her tight, like he would never want to let her go, without saying much.

At home, they went straight to bed. Oskar laid his head on Ester's breasts – the way he had always liked to do – and his hand on her belly. Lying in that dark room, only partially illuminated by a small candle and some dim lights coming in from the street, sadness overwhelmed both of them. Ester seemed extremely vulnerable, the self-confidence she had always brimmed with now entirely gone.

They were happy to finally be together. Ester whispered she hungered for that closeness, and that she was glad to know that Oskar was there if she needed him. She also admitted she was scared and that she kept thinking what it would be like if they decided to keep the baby: weather it would be a girl or a boy, and if they would be able to cope.

Oskar was thinking about the same, so he felt he should ask her once again if she was sure they had made the right decision. She quickly confirmed that she thought their decision was the best decision they could have made in those circumstances. She sounded sad, yet much more confident now.

***

Gentle circles around her navel. It turns her on. Or does it? Does she really want to make love in her state? I'm getting huge. Bizarre! Always thought a pregnant woman would leave me stone cold. Try to hide it from her. Keep massaging her belly, though. The excitement makes her body wiggle. But I'm not going to make another step! It would be inappropriate.

"Will you make love with me?" she asks with a hint of impatience.

"Err… Yes, if you want to," I smile a broad smile.

"Yes, I want. But please be careful."

I look into her eyes and slowly touch her voluptuous breasts. Kiss her passionately on the lips. Then the already rock-hard nipples. The well-pronounced areolas. I turn her onto her right side. Blow softly at the tiny hairs on the back of her neck. Kiss it. Squeeze her bum. Her waist twists and curves like a snake. I'll explode in a moment! Slide into her from behind. She moans. Her skin so sensitive to every touch. I turn her carefully on her belly. Her bum pale and amazing. Move in and out very gently. But it hurts her. She turns on her back and quickly pulls me back inside. I pulse like an open heart. Won't last long! She says I can cum inside her. I think I will. She brings her hands over her head, her legs spread wide and her knees bent. She draws them nearer the chest. I thrust her shallowly and gently. My left hand beside her right shoulder. My right hand massaging her labia and feeling each and every vain on my penis, coming in and out of her, mid-tempo. Again! And again! And I pull out!

We both sigh loudly, trying to catch our breath. And we smile. I explain I couldn't finish inside her. It would feel strange.

$$***$$

Two days later, we're on a plane to Bristol. It's a morning flight – the first one that day. We need to be in the clinic before 10 a.m. As luck would have it, across the aisle I spot two colleagues – a couple. I pretend I can't see them, but they can see us. I introduce them to Ester, and when they asks for the reason of our trip, we just say we need to organise something in Bristol. They're going to visit some friends in Bath.

In Bristol, we're surprised to find out that the clinic is on the far end of the city. I thought it said it was right beside the airport. But the taxi driver does his best to get us there on time – we tell him we're going to an important meeting – and when he does bring us on time, we tip him heavily, glad that we won't miss our appointment.

The clinic looks like a regular suburban detached house – maybe only a bit bigger. No signs there saying *For abortions this way.* Inside, the staff are very helpful and professional. We pay upfront and are asked to meet the doctor for the final consultation. I go with Ester to keep her company. The doctor goes through everything with Ester, step by step – including ultrasonography, which hits me right between the eyes – and ensures that Ester is under no pressure from anyone about deciding whether to keep the baby or not.

We decide on surgical abortion under general anaesthetic, as that is apparently the safest and most comfortable option. It means that Ester will be put to sleep before anything starts, and woken up after the procedure is over. I give her a big hug, and before she disappears behind the door, led by a nurse, it strikes me how innocent and child-like she looks in that white hospital gown. I hope she won't lose that innocence when she reappears in the same door two hours later.

I'm left on the sofa in the middle of the waiting room, with a heavily pregnant woman standing beside the reception desk to my right, and a teenage girl with someone who looks like her dad to my left. Two or three other people come in and out, but it's generally rather quiet.

Seconds feel like days, and it's impossible to concentrate on anything. I decide to go to Sainsbury's, which is just around the corner, for some groceries. But there, the only thing on my mind is how Ester's doing, and I can't get back fast enough. And when I do, the receptionist informs me that Ester's fine, but it'll take another half an hour for her to come round.

It takes less, and she does look fine. She's a bit dizzy, she says, but she's okay. We sit in a quiet corner, just the two of us, and we talk for several minutes to let her come to terms with what has happened, and to make sure that she really feels all right.

When it looks like everything is indeed fine, the receptionist rings us a taxi. A man in a black, unmarked sedan – "Secret service!" he laughs when he opens the door for us – takes us to our hotel beside the airport. Ester feels well, so we have lunch in a pub across the street. Then, we go to the hotel and cuddle up in bed without saying much. We just reflect on what we have gone through, or rather what Ester has gone through, and try to get some long-overdue peaceful sleep.

A DAY IN MAY

Style

"Any plans for the weekend?"

Ah, just shut up and do my hair!

"What's the weather like back at home?"

And give me something else to read – not the fuckin' Sun!

"Are you off today?"

Always the same bullshit, and always the same shitty papers. But I tip her anyway. She's not too bad after all.

I sling the bag over my shoulder, glance back at the chair to ensure nothing's left behind (please not the mobile again!) and shoot off. But a man in a dark suit and an ugly, purple tie, with a reusable Superquinn bag packed with some documents, blocks my way. I veer to the left, but he, too, veers to the left – which is to his right – and we almost collide. He smiles as if he wanted to offer me a drink, but I rush past him, towards Dawson Street, trying to avoid even the slightest eye contact. He keeps staring at me, though. I can feel it! The wanker!

What's the story with them carrying those shopping bags to work anyway?! Can't they just buy a normal man bag, a laptop bag, or a simple backpack? The black reusable Tesco or SuperValu bags, colourful cardboard gift bags, or those big paper bags from Arnotts or Clerys are here everywhere. Is that a Sunday family supermarket shopping trip or a morning rush hour? You wouldn't know!

Can you imagine living with such a man? When he leaves for work, you'd go: "And yer bag, sweetie! Don't forget! Oh, but there are still some spuds in it! Throw them in the fridge, will ya? And now come here! Give yer mama a big, juicy kiss before ye go, ye stud, ye!"

Love

On the corner of Stephen's Green Street and Dawson Street I bump into Julia. She's my best friend here. We used to be house mates in Beaumont – the only two 'normal' people there – and have been friends ever since.

Julia's from Austria. She's tall and beautiful, has long auburn hair, and now lives beside the Jameson distillery in Dublin 7. Works somewhere here, behind the shopping centre, for a small publishing company.

She's just gone out to run some errands, but it looks like she also feels an irresistible urge to tell me what I already know: that she's moving back to Austria next week. But she's in love, she says now. And that's new!

Right, she told me the other day, when we met in the Iveagh Gardens for lunch, that she fancied this guy, Robert, who'd done a few short in-house trainings for her company, and who – she'd quickly found out – she had plenty in common with. She'd chatted him up during a break, and then, one night, they'd happened to end up in the same pub.

There they danced, one thing led to another, and he was soon walking her home, holding hands. At the entrance to her apartment block he kissed her goodnight. Julia invited him for tea, but knowing that she shared, Robert didn't want to be a nuisance and so turned the invitation down. They agreed to see each other again, though. But the next morning Julia got sober and remembered that she was soon going back to Austria where a boyfriend was waiting for her.

"And Robert lives here!" she now exclaims in a whisper and blows her nose ferociously. Then she looks at me with those red, swollen eyes. Must have been crying all night. But didn't she say, on a number of occasions, that the spark between her and her Austrian boyfriend had long been gone? So what's the problem then? Doesn't want to fall for Robert for good and then be forced to leave? Maybe. But has she asked him to wait for her? Or to go away with her? She hasn't, but she doesn't explain why she hasn't. Might be afraid it's too early, that they haven't known each other long enough to start making decisions of this sort. But she doesn't really have to go back to Austria in the first place, does she? Kind of, she says, confused. It's not that simple – everything – apparently. And now she needs to run!

To MacNally Opticians beside the Shelbourne Hotel she needs to run. I've recommended that place to her, and particularly the manager there – Brian – who looks, and speaks, like Jack Black from Tenacious D.

But Julia wants to tell me all about Robert again. She's meeting a friend in the Czech Inn after work, and she suggests I join them for a girlie chat. I'm going to that thing in the Smock Alley Theatre later today, which is just around the corner from there, so I promise I will.

We give each other a quick kiss on the cheek and then split. I run down Dawson Street, and she goes her own way. Hope she won't end up under a car with those misty eyes.

From Dawson to Grafton

A man poses for a picture beside a Starbucks logo, though he looks like he doesn't want to be there at all. Fair play to him! Must have been his stupid girlfriend's – the photographer's – idea. Stand there right now or else there'll be no blow job! Poor chap had no choice.

But look! I've walked too far now! Duke Street is right before Starbucks, and I wanted to take that turn. Thinking about a blow job clearly makes me disorientated.

I go back and take a right into Duke Street, and then right again into the bustle of Grafton to grab my usual floss from the Boots pharmacy, and then that usual ruby red, beautifully smelling soap from Lush.

"Is it a gift, or is it just for yourself?" the girl at the till in Lush enquires.

"For myself," I say disinterested.

"Oh, great! It's nice to spoil ourselves once in a while!" she exclaims excitedly, almost as if she's just passed her Leaving Cert.

But it's just a piece of soap, isn't it? Is she made by her managers to come up with lines like that? They don't test their products on animals, but who knows, they might torture their staff into memorising pages and pages of customer-friendly, silly banter. Be as hip as hip one can be! And then try to be even hipper!

I cross the street in front of the main entrance to Trinity College, carefully wheezing through the oncoming traffic and struggling to avoid being inundated by a flood of tourists sporting Guinness Storehouse carrier bags. Why they all insist on visiting that place is simply beyond me. Some of them don't even like Guinness! A marketing wonder? No doubt. And don't get me wrong, I love stout, drink rivers of it (some ten to fifteen pints on an average week, and not only Guinness – also Beamish), but fondness for drink and making it number one tourist attraction in Ireland are two different things, aren't they? And all those kids who go to the Storehouse on their school or holiday trips – who approves of that? Why would they? And what happens with their free pints?!

Music

Moving away from Trinity, beside the Screen cinema on Hawkins Street, I pass a man who looks like Shane MacGowan. He also staggers the way Shane does.

I've been on this Pogue-mania ride again for the last couple of days. Been listening to their discography back-to-back, and even re-watched The Shane MacGowan Story with my fiancé yesterday. And this morning we danced like crazy to Greenland Whale Fisheries.

And now I spot this Shane look-alike, and I daydream that if it was a real Shane, I'd approach him and offer him a drink. He'd accept, and we'd walk into one of the pubs there (Chaplins or Mac Turcaill's) to talk about Ireland and poetry. And then I'd sneer in the faces of those friends of mine who keep saying that Shane is an old, sad drunk and lunatic, that he claims he plays Irish music with a band that's not even from Ireland, and that he tends to get so drunk that he throws up on stage.

Buahahah! But he recites poetry while they jizz over Twilight and upload pictures of their dinner on Facebook. So who's the real crazy one, eh?

Near Oranmore in the County Galway,
One pleasant evening in the month of May,

I met a damsel, both fair and handsome,
And she nearly took my breath away.

This country so desperately needs another Pogues, another band that would be original – not another clone or another lousy, poser shite played by hipsters who pay more attention to their hairdo than to their musicianship. A real band is wanted! A band singing about real life: about drinking, about fucking, about love. No more tear-drenching or politically correct bullshit that seems to spring from under every cobblestone of this city, a city flooded by doublespeak and over-politeness. I need balls, and I need them now! But I also need poetry!

If truth be told, though, I never have, and I never would really, approach a celebrity for an autograph – let alone for a drink.

Lunch

I pop into the bar on Burgh Quay for lunch and to catch up with a Polish friend who works there as a waitress. The place, as usual, is almost empty. Agata, the waitress, and another really tall and beautiful girl in my circle of friends, says there are rumours of a takeover. She worries heads might roll.

There are two other customers there apart from me – two Irish guys in their mid or late twenties, clad in boot-cut, scruffy jeans, dirty trainers, bright-coloured t-shirts and hoodies. Typical. Both look knackered. Half-empty pints of lager in front of them. One of them nods off with his head on the table. Must have been an all-night session.

Even though there are no other customers around, Agata needs to react. Lunch time's approaching, so a few white-collars from the local offices and the bank will probably arrive for a bite. And some will arrive for a drink. Like that middle-aged woman of shaky hands who, Agata once told me, pops in every second or third day to gulp two pints of Bulmers. That usually takes her no more than twenty minutes. Then, she sometimes rounds it off with a cognac. On the other days, Agata reckons, she frequents one of the pubs around the corner.

So, as I'm saying, Agata needs to react. She can't have people sleeping on the tables. The lads apologise and order another round of beers. But Agata refuses to serve them any more alcohol, and she politely explains why. She suggests coffee would be better. The lads keep trying to persuade her they're sober, laughing it all away, but as they see Agata getting increasingly impatient, they finally go for the coffee. And while she operates the coffee maker, I listen in on the banter between the lads.

"Hey! Don't sleep!" says the one who's less tired, trying to stop his mate from falling asleep again. "They'll kick us outa here!"

"Fook off! I'm not sleeping," mumbles the other one, slowly and dizzily raising his head and doing what he can to keep those tiny, red eyes open.

"Yes, you are!"

"Yeah, I am," he finally admits, "cos yer fooken borin, mate!"

Brats

After lunch, on my way home, I pop into Mace on Lower Mayor Street in the IFSC for some groceries.

Yeah, I know it's not the best place for that kind of shopping, but it's either this or the fresh food market in the square around the corner, though the market is open there only one day a week. Or Tesco delivery, but the service there is shite, so unless it's alco, mineral water, or toilet tissue, I stay clear of them. And yeah, I sometimes do feel guilty – for economic reasons, obviously – about not shopping at Lidl or Aldi, but I just can't stand those places.

I've been to Lidl once here, shortly after my arrival, and the number of sad faces I saw there outgrew – by far –

the number of sad faces in my local Lidl back at home. And people were supposed to be cheerful and happy here! It seriously made me feel dejected. And the soy milk I got there was leaking, and it fucked all the other shopping in the trolley! So I said fuck it!

But anyway, I'm now here shopping in Mace, and I spot those two brats by the deli counter there. Can't be more than eight or nine. In their inner-city brogues they order a sandwich each, hands in the pockets of unclean, grey, cotton tracksuit pants. Hair gelled. Fringes combed down flat onto their foreheads. Faces mischievous. And they can't stand still. Keep skipping from one leg onto the other, like they needed a piss – both of them. But they're also very picky. Takes them ages to decide what they want.

I meet them again later at the tills, their heads barely above the counter. Can see now that one of them is slightly older. And he pays for his sandwich first. Then he shoots off. The younger one is left behind. He throws the sandwich and a handful of coins onto the counter. But he's forty cents short, the shop assistant informs him indifferently. No pity there for the freckled boy. No good word. No turning a blind eye and pretending he's miscounted the coins. But I guess he must be excused, this shop assistant. He's been working here, at this very till, for years on end – at least since I moved to

Skellig House, the apartment block across the street, three years ago – so he cannot not be unhappy and frustrated.

The boy stares at the sandwich for a short moment, not knowing what to say or do. He then glances towards the door, perhaps hoping to catch a glimpse of the friend who might be able to help. That one has long been gone, though, so the kid drops his eyes towards the floor.

I swiftly dive into my wallet for the forty cents. Here! He lifts his head up, his eyes flooded, and he accepts the offer without saying anything. I don't say anything either. Just turn around and hit the road. But before I manage to leave the shop, I can hear the boy shout thanks loudly and cheerfully. I smile and head home. He runs like hell in the opposite direction, holding the sandwich tight.

All those street kids pretend to be so tough – they have to, I guess – but they need affection as much as any other regular kid does.

"Hey! Cheers! Thanks!!!" he shouts after me again before he disappears round the corner.

I like kids so much. I could sit back and observe them for hours, and never get bored. Their imagination and energy is just unbelievable. And it truly breaks my heart to see them neglected and abused. Their talents never discovered, their dreams never realised. And there are so many of them out on the streets here.

This particular one reminded me of one of the kids from The Tree of Life. Watched it a few days ago. Amazing film! Those close-up shots of the eldest son shortly after he's born must be one of the most beautiful shots of a baby in the cinematic history.

He also reminded me of this little chap, a seven- or eight-year-old complete stranger out of nowhere who approached me in the foyer of the Clarion Hotel in Cork a few months ago and asked, "Do you know what it feels like when you have no one to talk to? When you have no friends?"

He asked that question as if it was a perfectly normal question to ask a stranger, without the slightest hint of hesitation, so a few moments had to pass before I managed to get over the initial amazement and gathered my thoughts. And because I was suspecting him of rascally pulling my leg, I retorted in a rather curtly manner, "I don't really, no," and then added in the words of a Limerick hellraiser, Richard Harris, "I find myself the best company in the world!"

Feminism

Being increasingly interested in feminism, including active support of certain feminist organisations, I can't wait to attend the opening event of this year's Dublin Writers Festival, in the Smock Alley Theatre, where, in order to celebrate the publication of Fifty Shades of Feminism, a panel including a co-editor of the book, a journalist, an activist, and a theatre maker will talk about different aspects of feminism.

To my disappointment, however, the discussion quickly takes the path of the meeting I attended a few years ago – that of Atheist Ireland – with similarly high hopes, but which instead of a thought-provoking discussion occurred to be a joke-telling session. It was jokes about religious people then, and even though I'm anything but religious, they didn't make me laugh. Today, it's jokes and stories that aim at compromising men. And they are of similarly low standard. One of the panellists even goes as far as picking at her own son, comparing him to his older sister, and slagging him for being much less mature than his sister was when she was at his age.

I was expecting a reasoned discussion, a matter-of-fact platform for exchanging ideas, but instead I'm presented with a mixed bag of mockery and back-patting.

Funnily enough, some thirty minutes into the discussion, one panellist expresses her frustration at the fact that there are less than a dozen of men in the nearly packed theatre, which, she muses, must reflect how little interest Irish men have in women's rights. And soon after she expresses that concern, one of the few men in the theatre leaves.

He might have had various reasons to leave, of course, but the chances are high that he'd come here as a supporter of the feminist movement, but then he felt let down – if not appalled – by the whole spectacle.

As for me, I'm going to leave in a moment, too, since this is nothing more than a waste of time. Even the prospect of sitting in a pub and listening to Julia whining over her love affairs seems more interesting than this.

By the way, Julia is a PR specialist, and I wonder if any of these women here realise how big disservice they make through actions like this one to the movement that they claim to be part of. Unless they find solace in sitting over coffee and moaning about the status quo, there's something very wrong with their idea of spreading the message.

I'm off! Excuse me, madam!

Bars

I order this round. Two Heinekens and a Bulmers. The Bulmers is for me. It's been really warm lately, and in the summer I tend to drink more cider. I ask the barman to put loads of ice into the glass. Into the same glass, I mean, not into a separate one!

"But you're ripping yourself off by doing that!" he almost shouts, annoyed.

"I don't care! Just want Bulmers with ice – not a pint of Bulmers and a separate glass with ice!"

What am I supposed to do with that?! Pour the ice into the pint and splash the beer all over myself?! It's like every small drop would count to them. They fill up the glasses until they overflow, and then you can't even carry the pints back to your table without spilling the beer all over yourself!

Anarchism

On stage, there's a band getting ready for a gig. Among its members I recognise a guy from my yoga studio. Looks like some rockabilly thing, the band. Never really had a chance to speak to him, but once, when pulling on my shoes after a yoga class, I overheard him tell another yoga enthusiast how great the Occupy movement was. "It was a great opportunity to travel," he explained. "You had those villages set up in all major cities around the world. You could sleep there for free!"

Men

The next round is Julia's. She surprises us, though, as apart from the two Heinekens and a Bulmers (sure! a separate fuckin' glass with ice!), she brings two blokes. One is short and bald but rather well-built. The other one is taller, with black, slightly gelled hair and a rough face, though still rather handsome. Both around thirty.

While they introduce themselves, Julia whispers into my ear that they chatted her up at the bar and asked if they could join us. And they insisted on paying for the drinks. And she accepted! So now we're fucked!

The usual boring banter ensues: Where are you from? How long have you been in Ireland? Do you like it here?

The short one is unemployed, has been for quite a while.

"I smoke pot and watch movies all day," he says.

"Have you smoked today?" I ask.

"No."

"But you seem stoned."

The other one drives a waste collection truck. Says it's cool, especially on weekend nights, and especially when he works in Temple Bar, because there party girls always get into the driver's cabin and never want to leave.

But I have no problem with leaving. It's a very warm night, and it feels like real summer, though I don't really like summer. I only like it because then it's warm enough to sleep naked. And nothing feels better than hugging a naked, sweet-smelling piece of meet at night. Hope he's already waiting for me in bed.

UP!

1

Henri would often boast to his mates: "I love my French accent! It's great for pulling girls." But it wasn't this attitude that led to the break-up of his marriage – it was his beautiful wife who left him for a rather average-looking Irish banker. Henri swore he'd always been faithful.

He was born on the outskirts of Paris to a young Parisian nurse and a much older, Senegalese-born, Paris-bred entrepreneur. And he grew up to be a handsome young man, with a smile so dazzling that it could only be rivalled by the pure blueness of his eyes. He was well built but not very tall – his only inferiority complex.

And he was never much of a scholar, his highest academic achievement being a short postgraduate course in computing in one of those shady private colleges which these days every city is saturated with. That, however, didn't seem to bother him.

He got married soon after college, and because jobs were scarce in the area where he and his wife happened to live, and because both of them felt that good knowledge of English would benefit their careers, they soon decided to move to Dublin – a hub of IT services (for him) and pharmaceutical development (for her). Here they quickly found cosy jobs and improved their English to a decent enough level, but their marriage didn't last.

Our Henri got himself a nice girlfriend in no time, though – a gorgeous Russian blonde, Katya (short for Yekaterina). She was slightly younger than he was, had big, beautiful eyes and a figure like a model (in fact, she was a spare-time model). Henri was enchanted. Yet there was a problem.

2

Their first night together was planned perfectly – or at least it seemed to have been to Henri: he would collect her from work, she would come over to his place to take a refreshing shower and leave her things, they would then have dinner somewhere nice, after that a concert in Vicar Street, and then – finally – back to his place for the main attraction of the night.

Katya, however, had different plans. Instead of putting her clothes back on after the shower, she jumped straight into Henri's bed. He was somewhat taken aback by that unexpected turn of events, but – no surprise there – he was also very happy to see that Katya was screaming for him.

The thing was, though, he really wanted to see the concert, and to make both of them starve a bit. He wanted to build up some sexual tension and only let it explode after the candles have been lit, and not before his favourite Bordeaux has been poured into his favourite Bordeaux glasses. But Katya wouldn't wait. She wanted to be taken here and now.

It obviously didn't take her long to persuade Henri to skip dinner and instead head straight for cocktails, but – alas! – the ice pick seemed to be broken. She was lying there, waiting to be consumed, ready as ready one could be, but he just flopped as soon as he'd started pulling the condom on. And he became so tiny that it was embarrassing.

In order to give himself some time to regain erection, Henri started putting his tongue to use. And Katya repaid it by fellating him to the point where he got nicely big and hard. But no sooner had he torn another condom packaging open than his wand again lost its magical power.

And so Katya continued blowing him up, but once again he simply couldn't hack it. And now the three-pack of Durex bought for this occasion was gone.

They got dressed and went to see the second half of the concert at Vicar Street. On their way there, Henri explained that he'd never had problems like that before – not with his ex-wife, not with any other girl before her. It made Katya feel bad about herself, but he was quick to explain that it was solely him who was to be blamed.

Katya was very supportive and optimistic. She said they would try again after the concert, and she was sure everything would then be fine.

And they did, and it was. But Henri admits it wasn't easy to pull it off. He did manage to penetrate, but it was a far cry from his normal performance.

After that night, they would make love very often, and sometimes everything would be okay, but sometimes Henri would struggle. It felt like he didn't enjoy sex anymore, caused, most probably, by the embarrassment of the first night. It was lurking in the back of his head at all times.

3

Henri believed his sudden erectile dysfunction was a psychological problem, not a physical one. Therefore, without hesitating much, and without telling Katya, he decided to get Viagra. It seemed to make sense: the magic pill would give him an extra boost, they'd have a nice shag, and then – as a result of it – his confidence would return.

In the pharmacy, though, the pharmacist lady, trying hard but unsuccessfully to suppress the smile spreading visibly across her face, informed him that Viagra was only available on prescription. And the looks on the faces of the few people queuing behind Henry seemed to suggest that he was indeed the only one in there who didn't know.

He googled it and found out that the only male enhancement pills that could be bought over the counter were some dubiously effective substitutes. And as he wanted the real stuff, the very next thing he looked up was a men's health clinic. He would get the pill there.

4

Two days later, Henri sat in a big and very comfortable, smoky brown leather armchair, placed right in the middle of a stylishly decorated, though not very spacious, doctor's office in one of the townhouses on the south side, talking to an elderly gentleman tucked behind a heavy oak desk in front of him. Henri talked about his sex life. And it felt awkward. But he was determined to have the thing sorted out as soon as possible, so he didn't really care how it felt. He was actually proud of himself for having the balls to approach the issue the way he did – head on. And it did help that the doctor was a professional who knew exactly how to talk to his patients in order to put them at ease.

During the chat, Henri was asked many personal questions, but only one of them really made him think: Do you find your new partner attractive?

Henri said he did, without hesitation, but it got him there: Did he really?

Right, Katya was indeed stylish and very pretty, with luscious legs up to her neck, but some parts of her body, when released, were rather soft and saggy. And she had some ugly scars on her back, which initially was a bit of shocker for Henri, though he got used to them rather quickly.

What's more, she didn't have the slightest idea how to kiss. She would just throw her tongue out and whirl it like a windmill blade inside his mouth.

All in all, then, however much Henri might have hated to admit it, Katya wasn't a match for his ex. And therefore, for a short moment, he did start wondering if all those factors could have been the cause of his ED.

The other thing that the doc pointed out, and which was a no-brainer really, was that the simple fact of having regular sexual activity for a few years without a condom could have made him recoil at the mere thought of needing to refamiliarise himself with rubber.

The doctor then invited Henri onto the examination bed to ensure his genitals were in order. Pressing and gently punching his abdomen, the doctor slowly moved downwards. He pulled, pinched and squeezed, and as everything seemed to be beautiful there, he concluded that the only thing Henri needed was some time and peace of mind. He recommended taking things easy and being positive – that would soon bring back Henri's sexual stamina.

If the situation didn't improve, though, the doctor wouldn't recommend Viagra. In his view, young people all too often tended to make themselves dependent on it. He opined there was a more suitable treatment.

5

Henri was curious to know what the treatment was about, but when the doctor finally told him, the poor Frenchman almost fell off the big armchair that he'd moved back onto after the doctor's examination of his naughty bits. A series of injections directly into his willy wasn't something he would be much looking forward to.

The doctor knew perfectly well how gross the procedure sounded, so he only smiled a big, friendly smile and offered to show Henri that the whole thing was much less barbaric than it sounded. But before he invited Henri back onto the examination bed, he checked if Henri didn't have any major commitments that afternoon.

Henri didn't have any, so he was once again asked to drop his pants. The doctor prepared a syringe and told Henri to lie still. The injection wasn't supposed to be painful. But Henri was terrified! He observed in horror how the doctor grabbed the head of his mickey and pulled it downwards, towards his thighs, so that the part between the mickey and the pubic bone became nicely stretched, and then — *SMACK!*

The whole of the two-inch needle ends up in the base of Henri's cock!

It might have been a slight exaggeration, but Henri said it had looked like that famous adrenaline shot administered by Vincent Vega in Pulp Fiction in order to bring round Mia Wallace when she OD's.

Henri was so shocked that he didn't even make the quietest sound. The whole needle stuck in his membrum virile was not a pleasant thing to look at. It certainly made him pale and dizzy. Yet still, the doctor hadn't lied – somehow it wasn't really painful.

The doctor soon pulled the needle out and explained that a noticeable reaction was expected shortly. To help trigger it off, he wanted Henri to think about something nice. But Henri only laughed, suspecting that the old chap might have already forgotten he'd just stabbed him in his manhood. The doctor laughed too, but then he suggested Henri might want to help himself with a hand should there be no pleasant feeling spreading across his groin.

As it would feel somewhat awkward to start masturbating with the doctor sitting right behind the hospital screen, scribbling something in his notebook, Henri hoped for an automatic reaction. And, fortunately, when after a few minutes the doctor reappeared from behind the screen, he seemed contented with what he saw below Henri's waist.

The doctor then made it clear that the type of treatment that Henri had just experienced was recommended only in the most difficult cases. And although the injections were quite expensive, he insisted they were a much better solution than all the Viagra-type pills. They apparently cured, even those much older patients, giving them long-lasting results – not just short-term boners.

Before Henri left, the doctor had wished him – nudge nudge, wink wink – a pleasant evening.

And by god, Henri swore, was it a pleasant evening!

6

On his way back home, driving, Henri wasn't able to wipe out that evil, little smirk from his face when it had become obvious that his one-eyed wonder was unstoppable tearing its way out of the tight jeans Henri was wearing.

Later, when Katya finished work and came to his, they had long, dirty and satisfying sex. But however satisfying it was, it still can't have been enough for our horny Frenchman.

The next morning, at breakfast, Katya informed him that he'd woken her up in the middle of the night by masturbating in sleep. Watching him struggle, she'd reportedly asked if he needed a hand, but he then simply stopped fondling himself, turned around mumbling something incoherently, and just continued sleeping. And he now almost choked to death on his croissant when he'd heard about it. Laughing his head off, he tried to explain to Katya that next time she could go ahead and help him out without necessarily having to ask.

And there had been yet one other surprise waiting for Henri that night.

On his way back home from the clinic, he'd dropped by a pharmacy, but as he couldn't find his usual Durex there, he went for SKYN Mates. And only on his return home did he discover that he'd grabbed a size XL pack of Mates. But when a few hours later he got one of them on, what a relief it was! He felt as if he'd gotten himself a tailored-made suit.

He'd always struggled with pulling condoms on, blaming it on his clumsiness, clearly not realising that they'd all been too small for him. Yes, he said the women he'd been with would always make a comment, or two, about his size, but he'd never taken them seriously. After all, he'd sometimes compared himself to adult-film actors, however, he'd never been able to see any difference between his and theirs.

HERE TO STUDY, TO LIVE, TO LOVE

It was her first intercontinental flight, but Alejandra didn't have the slightest bit of worry. Maybe apart from the fact that all she could say in English was one single word: *water*. Difficult to believe, yes, but that's what she told me. Why hadn't she taken a short course before coming over? I don't know, I never asked. She might have thought she was moving to Dublin in order to learn English, so why would she study at home before coming here to study?

But it turned out she didn't really need English while travelling. Her connecting flight was in Frankfurt (Caracas-Frankfurt, Frankfurt-Dublin), where, with her German roots, strong Germanic features, long blond hair and a decent knowledge of the language, she felt like at home. In Dublin, during the passport control, when the officer realised she genuinely spoke no English, and when she showed him a letter from her language school, he let her go.

In the arrivals hall, Alejandra was met by an employee of the agency that had organised her trip to Dublin. She'd watched Taken before she decided to travel, so coming through an agency seemed a much safer option than doing it all by herself. After all, her father was a farmer – not a former commando. She didn't want to take any risks. The agency had looked after everything: the flight, the accommodation, the school. She'd bought herself peace of mind.

From the airport she was taken to an apartment in Mountjoy Place where she met her flatmates – three other Venezuelan ladies and two Argentinian men. And it was there that for the first time she'd felt things were not right. She'd come here to speak English, but apart from the big, red poster hung in the living room saying REMEMBER: PLEASE SPEAK ENGLISH! no one was speaking it!

On the other hand, though, Alejandra was happy to see she would be able to make friends so easily. She'd been worried that without English her social life would be rather limited in Ireland.

Ironically, she also appreciated the opportunity to share the apartment with all those people from different parts of Venezuela and, especially, from Argentina. It allowed her to break down at least some of the prejudices that South American nations – similarly to any other nation in the world – tend to hold against one another. She immediately loved all her flatmates, and with two of them she's remained close friends until this day – eight months later.

***

On the second day, the girls took Alejandra to Temple Bar. They wanted her to try Guinness and to see Dublin night life. It was a Friday night and the pubs were packed as usual. She enjoyed the lively atmosphere and the live music, but she found both Guinness and people's behaviour fairly strange. Her flatmates, who'd been in Dublin for a couple of weeks already, had told her about Irish women's peculiar sense of fashion, and warned her about men's – or women's, who knows?! – habit of breaking wind while in the company of others, but Alejandra's own observation was that even though it was still quite early in the night, most people were already pissed out of their minds.

She was also surprised that most men were glued to other men, and that women just kept talking to other women. There was not much mingling going on.

Yet the greatest mystery of them all was why so many people in a country as affluent as Ireland had such bad teeth. She wondered if it was because of Guinness.

That train of thought was unexpectedly interrupted by an obnoxious elderly man who was hanging around the same pub as the girls were, and who must have heard them talking, because when they were leaving, he suddenly bellowed, "Oh, Latino girls!" and pinched Alejandra's bottom hard, sticking out his saliva-covered, pale yellow tongue and wagging it like an old pervert that she was sure he was. It caused such a wild roar of laughter and ridicule among his pals that the girls were rendered absolutely speechless.

I was shocked! I didn't know what could I do! In my country I would hit him on the face, but here I haven't known how a people behave. I didn't speak the language, I couldn't fight! I felt like shit. After that we backed home.

***

After the weekend, on her first day at school, Alejandra was relieved to find out that she wasn't the only real beginner in her class. But, at the same time, she once again felt she was missing the point – almost everyone spoke Spanish there. The group consisted of four Venezuelans, three Argentinians, three Mexicans and one Spaniard. There was also an Italian girl on the list, but she would rarely bother to come to class. Alejandra had been expecting more diversity.

The two young Brazilian men who joined the group later that week, Bernardo and Marcelo, were therefore a real godsend. And apart from the much-needed linguistic variety, they brought in a dose of humour. It really helped Alejandra deal with the somewhat unusual situation she found herself in.

When the lesson started, for first time in my life I felt like a stupid. I was a manager in Venezuela, I had presentations important in front of fifty people, I teached at university. And here I couldn't answer simple questions about my day-to-day or hobbies.

The initial shock soon disappeared, though, and Alejandra started learning. And she learnt fast. She simply couldn't wait to reach the level that would enable her to start discussing some interesting topics – philosophy, relationships, et cetera – and to stop drilling how to buy a bus ticket or a dozen of eggs.

And it helped big time that her group was ambitious. They all spoke as much English as possible – also outside of the classroom – especially after the mixture of nationalities had been further diversified by the addition of two Saudi brothers, who, even though from a completely different culture, fit in pretty well.

The two Brazilians, however, wouldn't stop taking the mickey out of the brothers. Whenever the brothers weren't looking, the Brazilians would pretend to hold a bomb detonator in a hand, and while pressing down the thumb, they'd whisper, "Tick!" Everyone found it hilarious, including Alejandra, but inside she felt it was embarrassingly inappropriate. It was all supposed to be good-natured fun, though, she thought, and nothing that by any means was meant to offend the guys.

***

Alejandra had to leave the agency apartment not later than after the first three weeks of her stay in Dublin. In order to be able to work on her English, she was doing her best to find a place where she would be sharing with different nationalities. But that wasn't easy to organise – the language barrier was a problem. A vicious circle.

The other thing was that the many places which she viewed were of shockingly low standard, though very expensive nonetheless. And if some place was fine, the people who lived there seemed creepy.

Eventually, having virtually no other choice, Alejandra decided to accept the invitation to move in with the other Venezuelan girls from the agency accommodation.

They'd found a nice place in Parnell Street, above the McDonald's, but Alejandra wasn't very pleased to see that the merrymaking which had been an ongoing part of their life in the old apartment continued with ever-increasing intensity in the new one. If not wreaking havoc at home, the girls would go out and insist on Alejandra joining them. And sometimes she did, but most of the time she did not. She wanted to study. She only had that much money saved – enough for the duration of her six-month language course – and as she wasn't supported by her parents, she'd given herself mere ten weeks to improve her English to a level that would be good enough to start looking for a job. The money the job would earn her would finance her stay in Ireland for the following six months – until the expiration of her visa. But the girls kept coming back home late, laughing and chattering away, and falling over the furniture – and that included Alejandra's bed. As a result, she would often go to school half conscious.

And it wasn't just that she wanted to study, or that she had to save as much as possible – she simply didn't enjoy partying every night any more. She was a few years older than the other girls were, and she'd done it all before. She'd been living independently before her arrival in Dublin, whereas all the other girls had just left their family homes and now were going mad. Parties, men and shopping – or sometimes in the reverse order – were on their lips at all times.

***

Several weeks later, Alejandra thought it was high time to start looking for work. She still felt her English was rather poor, but she could see that people around her, with similar or even worse language skills, did have jobs. They worked as bartenders, waiting staff, cleaners and au pairs. And it was that last job that Alejandra wanted. It didn't result from the fact that she had such great love for children, though. No, it had more to do with the conditions in which she'd be living if she got the job: she'd be exposed to authentic language twenty-four seven, and, even more importantly, she'd be entitled to a room just for herself. Back in Caracas, she'd had her own apartment, so no wonder she was now getting increasingly fed up with sharing.

You try always to go up the standard of your life – not down, not to school time where people running and screaming, parties any time, and saying who go out with more Irish, and counting who kissed more guys during the night. I needed more quiet.

She logged onto some au pair websites and joined a few Facebook groups, but it was a friend of hers who in the end got her the job by recommending her to a friend of the Irish lady she worked for.

Alejandra was over the moon. She liked the job more than she could have ever imagined. She looked after a little, chubby boy – one of the sweetest things she'd ever had a chance to be around. He was incredibly affectionate, extremely polite and, as she would often describe him to her friends, very effeminate. They enjoyed spending time together so much that she didn't even mind looking after him after her working hours. And it was just herself, the mother and the boy in that big semi-detached house in the northern end of Phibsborough.

The school year ended soon, though, and so did Alejandra's contract. She was no longer needed. She had to find a new house.

But the plump boy wouldn't forget Alejandra so quickly. He'd often ask his mother for a permission to call her. And despite the fact that the calls weren't long, Alejandra always looked forward to them. "I miss you, Al," said quietly, almost in a whisper, just before he hung up, would bring a lump to her throat and fill her eyes with tears. She missed him a lot. After all, the ocean of love that was storming inside her, all the affection that she would normally give her family and friends back at home, had been transferred here onto the little boy.

***

With the experience gained in Ireland, finding a new au pair job wasn't particularly challenging for Alejandra. And it was just as well, because the stories she was hearing about her friends being paid half the minimum wage for very demanding jobs, or being asked for sex in exchange for employment, made her feel at least disappointed with how non-European citizens were treated in Ireland.

The mother did interview with me before on phone, and we were talking a lot in Spanish, but when she asked me go at her house, the father talked a lot. And it was like in a police room – he was very serious and checked everything on internet. "Where did you study?" "In Central University of Venezuela." "Where did you work?" "In a medical centre in Milla de Oro." "How long?" "And what did you like there?" "Why did you leave?" "Why did you come here?!"

But when I said him I was from Colonia Tovar, and that my grandparents were German, he changed completely, started smiling, very friendly. He told, "Oh, Alejandra! You're German! You're not Venezuelan." And I got the job. No problem.

The new job wasn't such plain sailing, though. In the traditional sense, this time it was a proper family – a mother, a father, two children (a boy and a girl), a dog and a hamster – but there wasn't much warmth and homey feeling to it. The parents did love the kids, but they didn't seem to have equally strong feelings for each other. And they had so little free time that the children were often left feeling lonely and desperate for at least a tiny bit of parental attention. Alejandra did what she could to make it up to them – especially to the girl who was four years younger than the boy, and who was always pining for some affection – but she knew perfectly well she would never be able to replace the mother. She also knew she would need to leave one day.

***

The two Brazilians who started school in the same week as Alejandra did, Bernardo and Marcelo, were less lucky work-wise.

Back at home, Bernardo had worked in finance – for a small bank, for a year or two. It was his first job right after college. And Marcelo had simply enjoyed himself, sometimes helping his family on a farm, but most of the time just playing the guitar and reading poetry. Here, he was only in Ireland because his best friend, Bernardo, had decided to come over and persuaded him to join in what was supposed to be the trip of their lifetime.

And it was. They first shared a room in a host family, but the family wouldn't talk to them, so they soon moved in with a Brazilian gay couple who were renting a two-bedroom apartment in Cork Street. But there, realising again that they wouldn't learn much English living with other Brazilians, or living together, they decided to split. Each of them moved in with a different host family.

They didn't move in there for a long time, though. In fact, they kept changing the families all the time, and for a number of reasons: because Bernardo would find something cheaper somewhere else, or because Marcelo would come across something closer to the city centre; because Bernardo's host parents would make love loud and often, and because Marcelo's host mother would let the dog finish off her meals straight from the plates, and then Marcelo would always find dog's hairs in his cereals.

But for work they looked together, walking around Temple Bar and leaving their CVs everywhere from pubs to restaurants to shops. They also created their profiles on a few websites, which was how Marcelo scored his first gig – as a cleaner.

He would scrub years and years of oil from the walls and ceilings of an army kitchen, wash blood- and urine-stained floors in hospital wards, and clean road signs covered in mud.

And it was that last job out on the streets that broke him. Last March, as you might remember, was particularly cold, and it was at five in the morning that Marcelo had to start work. His hands became permanently stiff and purple-red from the cold. How could he play the guitar?! It was even worse than that time when the boss hadn't bothered to give him rubber gloves in the army kitchen, and Marcelo got burnt with the chemicals provided for cleaning. But at least he got paid the minimum wage there.

Bernardo got just a fiver for holding a placard on Dame Street. And he was needed there only for a few hours twice or three times a week. But he still earned enough to pay for the lovely two-euro chicken baguettes from Centra, and the five-euro, home-made lunches in the Mezz, as well as the cans of Coors Light from wherever it was the cheapest, so he was happy enough. In Brazil, he'd worked full hours, but he couldn't afford much more.

The tracksuit-clad teenagers wouldn't let him be, though. He didn't seem too bothered with the rude comments they'd throw at him whenever they'd pass by, most of which he wouldn't understand anyway, but when one day they started beating him up, he had to abandon the placard and run away. He never came back.

***

In fairness, neither Marcelo nor Bernardo had to work over here. They did have enough money saved to support themselves. They had to. Otherwise, they wouldn't have been let into the country. The thing was, however, as in Alejandra's case, they wanted to stay here for as long as possible. And the main requirement to extend their visas was a receipt of purchase of another six-month language course, or any third-level course, which for non-Europeans wasn't cheap. And even if they hadn't been planning on staying here longer to study, going back home skint didn't sound like the best idea either.

Most of all, though, they wanted to party. They wanted to enjoy themselves. And they dreamt of travelling to all those places that people tend to travel to: London, Rome, Paris, Berlin and Barcelona. And then a few other places picked at random in Scotland, Holland or Belgium – the places to which they wouldn't have to fork out more than just a few quid for a return flight, a thing incomprehensible in South America.

And so they kept looking for a job. But apart from the job hunt, Marcelo was preoccupied with finding a way to make his former boss pay him for the last week of his employment in the cleaning company. He'd handed in his notice, but he hadn't got paid. And nothing seemed to work now to get him his money, until someone suggested contacting the guards or the Citizens Information Centre.

Bernardo, however, quickly managed to sort himself out with another job: door-to-door leaflet distribution. He was slightly worried about being attacked again somewhere in a dark corner of one of those housing estates that he and his colleagues were asked to bombard with fliers, but he was also happy that he would be walking a lot, for apart from mastering English, his goal here was to lose that extra weight that he had put on behind the desk in Brazil.

And he did lose a few kilos walking door to door, sticking his fingers through door mail slots, and once or twice running away from a fierce dog. But he also lost a lot of energy the way Marcelo had – trying to make the owner of the business pay him. Desperate, he looked for advice on Facebook, hoping some of the friends he'd made in Ireland could help.

Bernardo:

My boss didn't pay me Do you know what can I do?

Friend:

Have you finished work or are you still working for him?

Bernardo:

I don't know, because he didn't call me since last week

Friend:

Looks bad. Were you employed there legally?

Bernardo:

No. they pay me 4 euros per hour.

Friend:

?!?!?! Bernardo! Those guys prey on people like you.

Bernardo:

It was not legal

Friend:

I know it's too late to give you advice now, but you can't do things like that. How do you want to get the money now? If you go to the police they'll kick you out of the country because you worked here illegally.

Bernardo:

I didn't know about that... I couldn't go to the police

Friend:

There's Citizen Information Centre in O'Connell St. They have legal advice there, so you can go there. But you worked illegally, so I'd be careful if I were you.

Bernardo:

I think is better I don't go there   I'm thinking that the best thing is to go back to Brazil.

Friend:

Just don't let other people fuck you around. In Ireland things like that shouldn't happen. If you see someone paying less than what they should, kick their ass, or tell the police. Those cunts should be locked up!

Bernardo:

I know you're right. but I accepted this job because I was really in need

The rip-off entrepreneur wouldn't answer Bernardo's calls, but he did pick up when Bernardo's host mother rang him. She gave out to him like he was a little child, shouting in a high-pitched voice and threatening him with the Gardai. After that, it didn't take Bernardo long to find the full outstanding amount in his bank account.

***

After that unpleasant experience, Bernardo couldn't find a job for a long time. He was once again willing to work for half the minimum wage, but even those offers were nowhere to be found. One day, though, someone he knew in Dublin put him in touch with a Brazilian guy who worked as a gardener on a mansion in Sandymount. The guy was about to leave on a long holiday, and in order to ensure the job would be waiting for him, he was looking to arrange a cover. Bernardo was elevated when he heard about the opportunity, and until he saw his pay cheque, he couldn't believe he was earning ten euros per hour.

But it wasn't an easy job. And he would be needed there only once or twice a week, and, of course, always depending on the weather. Yet he liked it a lot. He also had a lot of respect for the owner of the possession – an elderly, heavily-bearded Irishman, and a real gentleman, who would often talk to him about Ireland, its history and its current political-economical situation. He also gave Bernardo great references and offered help with finding a new job when the other Brazilian came back from his holiday.

***

Marcelo envied his best friend's good fortune. After freezing his hands off cleaning road signage, and then tearing his hair out over how to make his ex-boss pay him, he fell out of the frying pan into the fire.

> *I worked kitchen porter. Job isn't too much bad, but I hated the manager. The boss is OK, but the manager is bastard. The boss is Irish, but the manager is Nigerian. He is really bad. One day he said me, "You are monkey." I said, "I know I can't speak English, but I'm not monkey!" I also worked part-time in hotel in Bray. Is OK. But isn't organised. One supervisor said me to come, and when I go, other supervisor is surprise and said they doesn't need me.*
>
> *But most funny, crazy job is my last job. Cleaning in B&B. In Drumcondra. Owner is gay, I think. He come when I cleaning kitchen showing him hand, that is pain in it, and*

ask me to... you know, bandage put on it. But he have no clothes. Have only towel on him... Around him. I feel strange, but say, "OK!" I quickly finish and he ask me if I make him massage. I say, "No! I need work, because will be late." He say, "Ehh, don't worry about work!" I say, "No, I don't know how make massage!"

But it's not finish now! Next day, I come to work and I start cleaning, but see one door open and he is on chair, you know, big chair, like sofa, naked with this... you know, this plastic pussy. You know! You put it on dick. And he is on chair with this and... Ahh! Crazy! So I go home quickly and never work there more.

✱✱✱

Alejandra's work life was rather uneventful compared with what her Brazilian friends were going through. But something important happened in her personal life.

It all must have started on her first day at school, yet it gained steam only a few months later – during a classmate's birthday party in the Mezz. Her teacher had also been invited (*Teacher, maybe we'll drink a vodka Friday? Go?*). He was around his students' age, or just slightly older, so no one found it inappropriate.

They were all immensely enjoying themselves there, their chatter and drinking accompanied by a band whose impeccable selection of rock'n'roll classics quickly got everyone moving, and it was in that growing excitement that Alejandra grabbed her teacher's hand and, without asking, pulled him after herself into the dancing crowd.

Even though by that time they both had already gotten themselves quite intoxicated on beer and whiskey, they still felt somewhat uncomfortable dancing like crazy in front of the other students pretending not to peep at them from behind their drinks. And it has to be said they danced rather closely – the way Patrick Swayze and Jennifer Grey taught them many years before (*I'VE HAAAD THE TIME OF MY LAAAAIFE!!!*). And they must have enjoyed it, because after the boogie their eyes would keep exchanging those knowing glances, and their lips would keep breaking into that little, mischievous smile.

But the teacher didn't seem too eager to offer another dance. Alejandra guessed it must have been awkward for him to do so when surrounded by his students, so when the time was right, she again took things into her own hands, and, as if it was just another harmless prank, she pushed him back into that whirl of naked arms and rocking hips in front of the stage, laughing and spinning like a twister under his arm, and often brushing his face with her long ponytail.

This time, to thank her for the dance, apart from a quick hug, the teacher also kissed her on the cheek. Back at home, kissing like that was nothing exciting – normal even among strangers – but she knew it must have meant something more in the land of touchless interpersonal relations, where even men refrain from shaking hands.

The band soon stopped playing, though, and the party had to move. It moved to the Workman's Club, where, while pushing their way through the crowd storming the bar area, Alejandra took her teacher by the hand, making it look like it was just for her not to get lost or left behind in the packed club. And she was happy to see that he didn't have anything against it. She even thought she'd felt his soft hand – almost twice the size of hers – sensually slithering around her fingers. But it could as well have been just her imagination.

The party continued, but all the dancing, drinking and chatting inevitably had to draw to an end. Alejandra and her teacher hung around, and when everyone else had left, they went for a walk.

The night was mild, and the Liffey motionless – as if devoting its entire attention to the full moon standing high in the cloudless sky, and to the colourful lights glowing from underneath the bridges and giving the town a fairylike feel. It made a perfect setting for a long, romantic stroll, but they drifted towards his apartment almost immediately.

I always talked with other students how nice he was, sympathetic and polite. But I also heard that he slept with his students and had a life of binges. Now I know it's not true, that most just was gossip, but I didn't know then, but also I didn't care.

In his home we started kissing, and he quickly started open my bra. I was a bit surprised, so I said him to stop. He stopped. But it was so exciting, and his smell made me crazy. I thought, "Fuck it! Tomorrow I worry about it." And we started kissing again and making love. It was really good. We had great chemistry.

The next morning he bought me a cupcake and coffee, and he walked with me to my home like a gentleman. But I still thought that it was for just one night, and was surprised that after that we started meeting and were together almost every weekend. I didn't understood. Of course I knew I was sexy, and funny, intelligent, but without the language I was like a stupid for him. I didn't know what did he want. Just sex? I don't know how good I understood what he spoke to me and how I answered the questions, but he always made me feel good, never ashamed. And soon I stopped worrying and been myself. At school he was very professional, but I liked to fantasise about jumping at him and making forbidden love on the desk after the lessons.

I finished school last month, but we still meet. And it's great. He's so much different, without labels. But I know that soon I will need to decide important thing. I don't want think about it yet, but soon I will need to decide about my future – stay here, or go back to Venezuela. I'm the youngest child and my parents are much old. My mother is sick, so I have a fear. I know I should go stay with them, or at least be in the same country.

But I love Ireland. Here I feel I live. I have time to live, and condition to enjoy it. It's not only work and work like at home. I know the job is simple, but I can explore new things here, like I always wanted. Experiencing, touching the world – not just looking at it outside a window in my office.

TOO FAR

For those who choose to walk alone

Nearly 9 a.m. Sunday. The alarm clock woke me up at 8.29 and then went off again after five minutes. And then again. And again a few more times. Just switched it off completely now. Hope I'm awake enough not to fall back asleep.

The radio's on. Phantom. Quietly. It was set for 8.30 in case the alarm clock didn't go off. A backup. I hadn't listened to Phantom for a few months, but now it's back on. I needed a break from it. It had been playing the same songs over and over again, and I simply grew tired of it. And I suppose I'll grow tired of it again in a few days.

I still lie in bed. Belly down. Trying to keep my eyes open. I usually stay in bed like this for some time before I get up, thinking about my plan for the day, or just listening to the radio. My girlfriend lies beside me, but we don't cuddle. She tries to get closer to me, laying her legs on my legs, and rubbing my left buttock with her warm hand. But I only twitch to let her know to feck off.

I took offence at something she'd said a week ago. Haven't spoken to her since then. Nor hugged her. But I love hugging! And so it's tough! And, of course, having no sex for a week is tough, too. And she lies here like this, half-conscious, wearing only knickers and a spaghetti-straps top, her hands and legs well warmed-up under the duvet. And she rubs me. It's not easy to stay offended!

But no! I'm not going there! To distract the thoughts of a good-morning shag, I start thinking about my trip. Right. Have to get up.

I draw back the curtains, slide the balcony door open, and lean my head out. It feels warm. Another cloudless day! Those cunts will have a nice bank holiday weekend alright.

They might then as well – eventually – stop complaining about the weather here.

By the way, the word *cunt*, said the Irish way, with a short but distinctly pronounced /u/ sound, has recently become my favourite word. So please don't mind me, and I promise I'll keep it to a minimum.

Judging by this cloudless sky, the forecast that I read a few days ago, which promised a beautiful weekend, seemed to be spot on. Actually, I didn't pay that much attention to it, but when I was walking along the walls of Dublin Castle later that day, on the corner of Little and Great Ship Street, I overheard an elderly chap telling a friend about it. They both rubbed their trembling and deeply-wrinkled hands in anticipation.

It wasn't very warm that day, though. I was wearing only a jumper, and when I got to Dubh Linn Gardens to read a paper, around 11 a.m., the wind was so chilly that I had to shield myself behind the bushes and the flowers, and the snake-statue fountain which bubbles every couple of minutes in that secret little spot between The Coach House and the Garda offices. But today looks like it'll be really warm.

"Where are you going?" asks my girlfriend quietly, as if she wasn't sure if she was allowed to ask.

"On a trip," I say, confidently.

"Can I go with you?" she asks.

I say she can't, but it breaks my heart. It would be so nice to go together. But I've decided I'm going by myself. I'm not giving in at such an early stage. I'm still offended. Has she forgotten already?

***

I sat down with a map last night and decided: Balbriggan. I want it to be a short trip. Don't want to go far. I can't. If I could, I'd have already gone yesterday for a weekend trip. But I had to work. I also have to work tomorrow, so I don't want to come back home very late. Another reason is that I'm broke. If I wasn't, I might have decided to go to Wexford – supposedly the sunniest place in Ireland, and sporting the most beautiful beaches – but that would have meant a longer, more expensive trip. And so it is a short trip to the north.

But first – breakfast! A big one, 'cause I realise I may not have proper lunch today. Soy sausages, a fried egg, baked beans, a tomato, some bread, coffee and some orange juice.

As soon as I'm finished with it, I look for a pair of black sandals. But I can't find them anywhere. Must have left them back at home last summer. Might have thought I wouldn't make any use of them here. Have to take black

Converse trainers instead. Before that, though, I put on my favourite army trousers, a khaki t-shirt, and a black hoodie. And a khaki military cap to match. But I don't pull it on just yet. It's in the bag, waiting for the sun.

***

It's 10 a.m. now and I walk briskly through Temple Bar. There are few people around, and most of them seem to be tourists. It's not very warm yet. I'm happy I don't have the sandals on.

Millenium Bridge takes me across the Liffey and lets the morning breeze run a chilling shiver down my spine. I turn right after the bridge and walk along the Liffey Boardwalk past the usual number of junkies. There are also a few non-junkie types who, already half naked, look towards the sun rising above the old buildings on the quay across the river, impatiently waiting to have their skin covered with a summer glow.

I turn into O'Connell Street, get to the Spire, and then right into North Earl Street and Talbot Street. There's a Tesco there, so I pop in to grab The Sunday Times, a one-litre Ballygowan, and an oats snack bar.

Five minutes later, I'm at Connolly Station, with an eight-euro return ticket in my pocket. As expected, the station is full of sun-deprived individuals who wish to make the most out of this beautiful day somewhere outside of the city. Hope not all of them are going to Balbriggan!

On my way to the platform, I hear a tourist – American? – voicing her opinion on how reasonable the cost of public transport is in Ireland. Her companions agree. And I agree too, I think.

I have 20 minutes left. The platform is loud with cheerful conversations and the swish and screech of the passing trains. Most of the gathered folk jump on the Howth train, which comes first. Cool! But plenty are still left for what seems to be the one to Drogheda – through Balbriggan. Not so cool! I was hoping I'd be able to sit comfortably by the window and do a bit of sightseeing.

I've been to Drogheda before, but I only had a quick glance at it through a car window then. I and my girlfriend were on our way to Belfast and decided to stop over either in Newgrange or in Drogheda. We went for the latter one, but when we got there, it had started lashing. So we just drove around the town and then left. Should go there properly one day.

I sit down on a plastic bench next to a family of four. The mother stands, gazing afar off. The father and two children, a boy and a girl, sit. They're all dead silent. I pull the newspaper out of my bag. Wouldn't have bought it today had it not been for the DVD of A Portrait Of The Artist As A Young Man – part two of the James Joyce's collection. A week ago there was a screen adaptation of Ulysses. Good stuff! Bloomsday's in two weeks!

I wouldn't have bought the paper without the DVD, because now I try not to buy more than I'm able to read, or at least not significantly more. I realise I should have taken one of the papers or magazines from the pile of last month's publications left on the chair in the bedroom. Or perhaps something from the previous month's heap of magazines stored in the box beside the TV stand. Or I might have opened the storage in the hall stacked high with last year's mags. Or maybe one of the books bought and swiftly abandoned on the desk by the window. Never read, never appreciated. I'm sure they've already lost the last hope to ever be touched again. Good they don't know I was looking at some other books last Friday in the Chapters bookstore in Parnell. I was on my way back from the dentist and simply couldn't help entering the shop. It always amazes me how many books they've got there. And it was so hard not to give in to the temptation to help myself to a few titles. I actually ended up in the photography section looking at some books of erotic photography. I did! Seriously! Because I now have this idea to cover one of the walls in the bedroom – the one behind the bed – to cover it in erotic photography. But only the most sensual stuff there – no hard core. Actually, there are already quite a few nice pictures hanging there, torn out of a few photo magazines, as well as a catalogue I recently bought at the Centre Pompidou in Paris. So, when I saw those books in Chapters, I thought I'd buy one of them. But then I remembered another book of collection photographs that I'd bought in Paris, which is something like five hundred pages, and so I forced myself to promise to myself that I wouldn't buy anything else before I go through that one.

"Are we going to move all of them?" asked my girlfriend pointing at the six bags that I'd packed to the brim with papers and mags the day before we moved to our new place two months ago. But it wasn't a reproachful comment – rather a humorous one. And yet, I believe, one that was supposed to make me think about what, apparently, had become my problem. And it did. But I still didn't hesitate to retort, "Yes, we are. I'll read them all!" She only burst out laughing, though, as that was exactly what she'd been hearing for months on end. And it had always made us laugh. There was no way I'd ever find enough time to read all that – even if I was unemployed and without a hobby for a year.

But it did indeed make me think, and a decision was made to sort all the newspapers and magazines, to take with us only the most interesting ones, and to get rid of the rest. I was actually surprised – and a bit embarrassed – at how many papers there were in there, untouched, still folded in half, even though some of them were well over a year old by then. Half of them were The Irish Times, and mainly the Friday edition with The Ticket. I decided to quickly leaf through the lot and tear off all pieces by Michael Harding and some by John Waters to read later. I also wanted to keep all the articles reporting on the IRA and the Troubles, and on the whole peace process, and everything else on Irish history – all the things that I'd been researching since my arrival in Ireland. Oh, and I'd also glance through all the things about immigrants, 'cause it's always interesting to see what they think about us. The rest was thrown out – tens of kilos of it. Pity the recycling system was so poor in that place. Everything had to end up in the same bin – be it stale food, plastic bottles, glass jars, old clothes, and the papers. Do they sort that stuff later them cunts? Doubt it.

***

The train is full. No chance to sit by the window. An aisle seat will need to suffice. Beside a red-haired, pale-faced guy, clothed in a cheap, black uniform. Must be on his way back from work. Looks knackered as hell. Tries to sleep.

As the train leaves the station, I look to the right – towards the docks. There, the old and ragged Dublin of small, red-brick terraced houses rubs shoulders with the business world of glass walls and modern architecture. As strange as it may sound, it does look nice. And it will look even nicer when the few things that are currently being built there are finished: the sloping cylinder-shaped Convention Centre on the north side, and Grand Canal Square with its theatre and a red-carpet walk on the south side, the two new bridges, new canals and urban parks. And the Point Village. And the Luas red line extension. Bollix! Is it two years now since they started digging!? Might be even more than that! But once the line's finished, it'll be much more convenient to live there. After all, you can't depend on the bus service in this city, can you? It's been almost two months since we moved out of the IFSC, but, who knows, we might be back there one day.

In the seats in front of me, but facing the other way, two women talk. English is not their first language, though they're very fluent. They talk about work. The one sat by the window has long, curly, dark hair tied in a bun. Beautiful. This, unfortunately, is all I can see from behind the seat. To see her face, I peep through the gap between the seats. She seems quite young, probably in her mid-twenties. And she's rather dark-complexioned. Very pretty. Can't see the other girl, though.

We pull into Portmarnock Station, and some people get off. Then Malahide, and more people leave. Two seats become available on the left-hand side of the aisle, so I take them. And now it's more comfortable. I enjoy the view over the bay. But to my right I can now see also the second of the two girls. Her complexion is even darker then her friend's. They might be Spanish or Italian, but I can't spot that typically strong Spanish or Italian accent in what they say. They seem easy-going and well-educated. It would be nice to talk to them for a while, but I'm not the type of guy who all of a sudden starts talking to strangers. I do admire those who can do that, but I'm definitely not one of them. I'm a shy, sad cunt.

I still look to the right, but now I stare at the easternmost point of the Republic – Lambay Island (just googled it on my Nokia – that's how I know). It looks beautiful in this amazingly sunny weather.

The next stop: Skerries. The tired guy still sleeps, and the girls have now stopped talking. They travel further. And so am I, but only to the next station. According to the road map that I took with me, there's a sandy beach there in Balbriggan which stretches as far as Dundalk Bay – sixty or so kilometres north of Balbriggan. I want to spend the day on the beach, doing nothing but relaxing, reading, and having a bite of something nice to eat.

***

The train approaches the town, rolling over the bridge, at its foot a sandy beach bathed in the morning sun. Looks like a decent spot. It's also the final stop for the tired guy and the girls. The train comes to a halt. I don't rush. I let the ladies go first. We all go through a small, dodgy-looking station building out onto the town. No one checks the tickets. And as I walk out of this tiny building, the girls turn around and head back. "We have to ask someone," I can hear the curly one say. Ask me! They won't. But I don't know where to go either. I keep walking down the street anyway, though. I guess it's impossible to get lost in a town like Balbriggan. I follow several other people who have just gotten off the train.

One guy veers to the left towards something that looks like a small passage under the railway track. It might lead to the beach, but I decide to head to town first. I want to have a quick look around before I hit the beach. And it is a typical, small Irish town with miniature, grey and densely built terraced houses, narrow streets, and friendly-looking people.

I walk down Railway Street and then turn left. I walk on the shaded side of the street and suddenly realise I've forgotten to check the train timetable to make sure it's the same as the one on the Internet – just to be on the safe side! Not like on that cold October night last year when I was left waiting at Wicklow Town Station for well over an hour, 'cause I hadn't checked the timetable. The station was deserted, bar a drunk who had popped in to entertain me with his drunken songs. And there was no coffee shop around where I could take refuge in, nor was there a takeaway to get a bag of chips.

I hesitate for a second whether to go back to the station and check the timetable, or to have faith in Irish rail and just continue climbing the curved road in front of me. I can't really be bothered in the end, so I go for the second option, and then start following a narrow, almost completely dried-out canal which takes me to a small park. It's still quite early in the morning and maybe that's why the park is almost deserted – there's only one man there and one German shepherd that the man belongs to.

Here a light summer breeze touches my face. I look in the direction of the sea, but the view is obstructed by a tall bridge. It's the same bridge that I crossed on the train 15 minutes ago.

I walk under the bridge onto a huge beach. The sea is very far out. There are a few people running around, screaming and splashing the salty water all over themselves and all over each other. To the right, there's a pier and a lighthouse, and a boat lying on its side, partially sank in the sand. I go nearer. The sand is rather hard and wet, but as I get closer to the pier, it gets really muddy. I keep my trainers on. I don't want to walk into some shit barefoot.

The lighthouse is quite neglected, its plaster coming off. Doubt if it's still in use. The boat lies right beside it, on the beach side of it. It stinks. It's rusty and covered in disgusting seaweed. Strange someone's left it like that here. Must have been a while ago.

I now look to the right and spot several other fishermen boats there. But those are properly roped to the pier, and even though they look dodgy, I reckon some poor bastards might still need to carry them to the sea. I take a few pictures.

I reverse and head back onto the main part of the beach. A small group of kids run around there, jump into the sea and then back onto the sand, laughing their heads off. I smile at them and take off my trainers. And I take a picture of the trainers covered in mud. I also photograph my pale feet. Why? Just for the craic. Then I lace the shoes together, roll up my trousers well above the ankles and with the tips of my toes decide to check out the water. It's fuckin' freezing!

$$***$$

At the far end of the beach I can see a small grassy ascent with a round tower on top of it, and big rocks down beneath it. With time on my hands, I decide to explore the tower and see what's further behind it.

As I walk towards the tower, I can feel the sun getting stronger. I take the hoodie off and put the cap on. Under my bare feet the beach gets rockier, but I struggle on. The rocks soon get much bigger, though, and there are now so many of them that I just need to start balancing on them instead of trying to walk around them.

And now I'm bent in half – and it's not just because of the pain that my feet endure on these sharp rocks. I simply need to ensure I'm ready for a fall, which I bet will come sooner than later. But when another piercing pain shoots through one of my feet, I finally surrender and put the trainers back on.

Two young lads stare at me from a dune afar, and I bet they wonder what the hell is wrong with me. But I just want to see what's behind the ascent. Pure curiosity – or rather a zest for adventure. Nothing else. And it's easier now with the trainers back on. Some of the rocks, though, are covered in slimy seaweed, so I need to be careful not to slip. It smells bad and there are ugly bugs everywhere.

When I eventually reach the ascent, and then go round it, the view is absolutely tremendous: the beach is wide and the sand is blinding. And the area is almost completely deserted. Far, far away, a tall cliff stands proud.

The sand is much softer here, so I swiftly bare my feet again. The hoodie back on, though. The sun is scorching and it seems like quite a long walk is in store for me if I want to explore that shiny cliff far on the horizon. I don't want to get sunburn or – even worse – sunstroke.

As I walk towards the cliff, I spot a family of four sitting together on a big blanket. They stare at me relentlessly. And they might be right: they're there sunbathing in their underwear while this guy walks along the beach in military trousers and a black hoodie – like a lunatic. But I don't care. I focus on this very moment and take pleasure in strolling barefoot in a zigzag manner into and out of the sea. It's fabulous. I ponder life, its simple pleasures, my relationship, the fact that I'm so fucking stubborn, and that my girlfriend is so great putting up with the sulks and swings in my mood. I also notice that I start feeling peckish. I'll have a picnic on the cliff as soon as I get there. And I get there in no time, quickly finding a shady spot up on the grassy side of the cliff. Spreading a small blanket on the grass, among the small bushes and moors, I stretch out my legs and let out a huge sigh of relief. The breeze is lovely. It cools me down. Seagulls cry loud, circling above the sandbank. And I'm more than happy to be sitting here like this, free to do what I want, and having the peace and quiet to think.

The cliff brings back memories of the cliff that I unexpectedly ended up discovering last year, when my parents came to visit. As it was already their second trip to Dublin, this time I wanted to take them somewhere outside of the city. And because my dad is a vivid mountaineer, I picked the area with the highest mountains – County Kerry.

We drove to Tralee, where we stayed overnight, and the next day we headed for Mount Brandon – the highest mountain on Dingle Peninsula. And even though we weren't able to find our way to Brandon, it didn't really matter – there were plenty of other high mountains all around us. The views were amazing, and it didn't rain.

After hiking for about two hours, we reached one of the lower summits. Behind it, apart from a herd of sheep guarded by a mean-looking ram, we found a massive field of windswept moors. I was enchanted and immediately started exploring the field. And I encouraged my parents to follow me. I had a feeling that in the place where the field ended, far from where we stood, but still reachable, there would be cliffs looking out onto the Atlantic.

The old folks did start to follow me, but they were rather slow, so the distance between me and them quickly increased to the point where verbal communication became impossible. In the meantime, only to make the whole experience even more interesting, the soil under my feet started getting plashy. And as I was taking in the enjoyment of it all, I heard my parents calling from the distance and gesturing to turn back. They'd had enough and were retreating. Their boots must have been less water-resistant than mine were. But I didn't want to go back now being so close to what looked like the very end of this island, so I ignored them. I started running in the opposite direction, jumping over big curbs of bog that had sprung across the field like big mushrooms – had someone cut turf there? – and splashing water from under my boots. It reminded me of Bear Grylls running around like this in that episode of Born Survivor where he's cast away the west coast of Ireland. You seen it? Total exhilaration!

After another curb of bog, which I didn't hesitate to leap over straight into the wild heather behind it, I found it: the incredible vastness and the endless blue of the Atlantic. The mighty cliff was only a few metres away. I crept to the edge of it and lay on the blanket of purple heather and green moss. The cliff was huge, but not as steep as the Cliffs of Moher – more like the cliffs in Howth. I lay there and looked down at the waves hitting hard at the rocks below. And even though the wind was blowing mercilessly, the place felt wonderfully peaceful and quiet. I would have loved to be able to stay there for hours, just lying like that and enjoying nature in its rawest form, but I knew my parents were far away from where I was, and probably already worried sick, so I quickly took a few pictures, recorded a short video, and ran back.

***

There's still not even the tiniest cloud in the sky, and the sun is still blinding and piercing. A couple walk below the cliff holding hands. I open the bag and pull out some fresh bread and a box of beans that I bought yesterday at the organic market in Temple Bar. The market is there every Saturday, and I always make sure to pop in. The red pesto and the green wild-garlic pesto they sell from one of the stalls there is amazing. The beans are not too shabby either.

I also pull out The Sunday Times and, surprisingly, go straight to the sports section – surprisingly, 'cause I hardly ever read about sport. But Leinster won the Heineken Cup last week, and it's still all over the papers, and I want to have a look, 'cause the lads really were great: a grand slam in the Six Nations two months ago, and now this. Those victories, along with the beautiful weather, seem to lift everyone's spirits out of the gloom and doom of the recession, and to help forget, at least for a moment, about the horrors and shame of physical and sexual abuse inflicted on thousands of Irish children by the Christian Brothers and numerous other religious orders, which has recently been revealed in the Ryan Report.

It was amazing – the Six Nations Championship. The final kept us with the hearts in our mouths all the way throughout. When Wales didn't manage to get that kick over the crossbar in the very last second of the game, the outburst of joy was wild. We had a small group of friends over in Dublin that weekend, and even though they understood nothing from the game, they loved the whole atmosphere, mingling with both the green jerseys and the red jerseys in O'Neill's.

I now take out a map and try to figure out whereabouts I am. Must be somewhere halfway between Balbriggan and Gormanston. Guess it would be rather boring to walk exactly the same way all the way back to Balbriggan, so I reckon I'll just continue walking along the beach till I get to Gormanston. There I'll catch the DART back to Dublin.

It's only 2.15 now, so it shouldn't be too late for the last train when I get there. But before I climb down the cliff to recommence my journey, I have a Kellogg's Nutri Grain apple bar for desert. Nom nom!

From here, the beach is an almost perfectly straight line all the way up to the very horizon. And on the horizon – far, far away – there's a big, shadowy thing. I have another look at the map and guess it must be the mountains between Carlingford and Newcastle in Northern Ireland. But I'm amazed I can see them from down here – according to the map, they are at least sixty or seventy kilometres away. And they look amazing bathed in the searing sun and veiled by the steam hanging over the glittering sea.

I now try to walk a bit faster to make sure I get to Gorm... Gormsomething on time. The beach gets slightly narrower. And I spot a cow looking at me from a not very high dune covered with tall grass. I look at her, too, and I take a picture. She doesn't take a picture of me, though she seems to smile.

The journey eventually starts getting a bit tedious. I'd like to be there already (Are we there yet?! I've no one to ask!), sitting on the beach and having a nice, fresh ice cream, or a refreshing fruit salad. My feet start hurting. All the walking and rock jumping now begins to take its toll. But I don't want to sit down again – firstly, there's no shade here at all; secondly, I've no idea how far it still is to Gorl... Shit! I keep checking the name, but I still can't remember it. Map. Right! Maybe this time: Gormanston!

I go round another small, grassy bump, and there I immediately notice something on the beach in the distance that reflects the sun. I get excited! Guess my destination is not as far away as I thought. And as I get closer, I can see many more beams of sunlight being reflected from some objects on the beach. UFOs? No, it soon becomes clear: the beach is packed with cars. It actually looks like one big car park right on the beach.

But now, here, under my legs, there's water all over the place. I look right, then left, and then around myself, and I quickly realise I'm in the mouth of a river. It's almost dried out and seems small enough to cross, but I'm not sure whether it wouldn't be better to veer to the left and try to find a bridge. Ah, fuck it! I pull up my trousers and go for it. And, luckily, the water level never really gets higher than slightly above my knees. It's disgusting, though. My imagination fucks with me terribly, projecting the worst possible images: those of smelly, green slime full of ugly water creatures and long eels sliding between my toes and wrapping around my ankles. But the chatter and laughter of the kids playing at the other end of the mouth pulls my mind out of the nightmarish scenarios and gives me some courage to wade on. If there were brutal monsters hiding in here, then I'm pretty sure those kids would have been eaten alive long ago.

When I eventually manage to get out of the water, I'm shocked – there are cars everywhere. Some people sit inside, with the windows and doors open, others sit beside the cars. Kids run around screaming. A small group of twenty-something drunks act the maggot with a football, kicking it as hard as they can even though there are a few dozen people, and cars, around them. I hope they hit one of the SUVs and some well-built lad comes out of it and pounds the snot out of them – or at least tells them off like little brats that they are. The ball inevitably hits one of the cars, but the unfortunate footballer just shouts *Sorry!* and simply keeps on playing and laughing. No one kills him.

The sand here is very hard and dark. It sure is more comfortable to sit in a car. I spot some steps over the dune leading out of the beach. I climb them past some teenagers drinking beer on a grey stone wall. Two of the girls chat away, whereas the other girl makes out with her fella as if they were all alone somewhere cosy and isolated – like behind one of those dunes that I went past an hour or so ago. They might be unaware of the existence of those places, so I hesitate for a second if I shouldn't share my knowledge with them. They could get off properly there.

Reaching the top of the dune, I walk past a small car park, which is almost empty (Sure, all the cars are on the beach!), onto the main street. It's busy as hell – like in some holiday resort in the Mediterranean: kids run around shouting and laughing; men and women in shorts cool themselves with ice-cold beer, fizzy drinks and fruit ice cream; and the elderly sit on the benches, absorbing all the energy that the summer sunshine can give them. No, actually, looking more carefully now, I realise most of the elderly hang around the pub beside Paddy Power's. I want to approach them and ask for directions to the train station, but their red faces and tired eyes scare me off. I decide to grab a fresh ice cream and gather some courage first.

I get the ice cream from an ice machine parked by the main road. The ice cream seller informs me that the station is a five-minute walk from where we are. I take the ice cream, immediately devour half of it, and then walk in the direction that he points – up a small hill past a local shop where some kids hang around eating crisps and drinking Powerade.

The station is right there, around the corner. I look at the timetable and notice that something is clearly wrong – it says *Laytown*. What the fuck is Laytown?! I look at the timetable again and scan the list of stations, but I can only see chaos there. Nothing makes sense. I take out the map. No! I grab the phone and look for the GPS application that I hardly ever use. I ask it for my current location. It gives me *Laytown*. But where the hell is Laytown?! I zoom out. Then zoom out again, and, yeah, right, Gormanston is there too, but way down below – towards Dublin. I look at the map, and it says the same: I must have gone past Gormanston a few hours ago. But there were no houses there that I could see from the beach. None! Apart from the cow, there was nothing. But maybe I shouldn't have expected anything more than that in the first place? After all, it's a farming country, isn't it?

***

The train leaves in around 45 minutes, so I decide to go back to the beach and people-watch for a while. The sun is not as strong as it was earlier in the day, but the beach is still packed. Most people are already red like a fire engine (Shhh! I was taught this simile in my English school!). They'll be fucked tomorrow. When you look at them lying around sunbathing all day like that, none of them being used to this type of sun, and, I'm pretty sure, only few of them giving a shit about sun lotion, it's no wonder Ireland has one of the highest rates of skin cancer in the developed world.

I sit down on the stone wall across the steps from the teenagers. They have now stopped licking each other. The lad sits on the wall, and the girl stands between his thighs, her arms thrown over his shoulders. They talk. All of them. It must have been pretty awkward for the other two girls to witness all that making out.

It was like on that camping holiday with my girlfriend and a bunch of friends when I was eighteen or nineteen. One night, by the fire, we were drinking beer under the stars, and apart from me, my girlfriend, and two male friends of ours, there was a girl who had come camping with her parents, but who had been invited by one of the lads to join us that night by the fire. And it was burning like mad, well maintained by one of the beach changing rooms that we'd violently dismantled, under the cover of the night, to use as firewood. At one point, even though I don't like kissing in public places, I jumped at my girl. And after a few moments, when we paused to take a sip of beer, I noticed the guy who had invited the girl was now kissing her too. At the same time, I became aware of the fact that the other chap was sitting there all alone, staring hard into the fire. He must have felt totally dejected sitting there like that on such a lovely night, beside two couples sucking the tongues out of each other's heads. I would have hated to be in his shoes, so, out of solidarity with him, never again did I kiss my girl that night by the fire.

Now I still sit here on the wall, and this beach full of people reminds me of The Van. I saw it a few weeks ago.

Never read the book, though. A very good comedy, and Colm Meaney is again great as a mean as fuck cunt. I think I haven't seen a film with him where he'd play a different type of character. Maybe in Star Trek he does, but I haven't seen Star Trek. Anyway, each time I think about The Van, I think: chips! Fat, ugly, salty chips! I've had them almost every day since I watched the film. And yes, I want them now too!

I take a look around, but there's no chipper on the beach as far as I can see. I need to go back into town. But here now, right in front of me, I spot a Garda, or rather some kind of beach-safety officer, on a bike. I'm curious how far it is to Gormosomething. "Gormanston?" he asks. I nod. He hesitates for a second and then shoots, "Around 7 miles." I thank him politely, but I think he must be out of his wits! Eleven fucking kilometres I walked?! And that's only from Gorm? Never! Impossible. Must have got his numbers wrong.

Apparently people in this country cannot count. And although I'd always disregarded similar statements as being a bit of an exaggeration, some gibberish coming out of the holes of envious immigrants who will never miss an opportunity to pick at the Irish, who claim that even the managers here are no exception – that they are an uneducated bunch unable to perform even the most basic mathematical equations, but the guy who served me at the fruit and veg stall at the Temple Bar market yesterday did have some genuine problems. Well, OK, truth be told, he was already quite drunk, even thought it was just after 4 p.m. And when I wanted to pay 2.70 with a fiver, he put his hand into a wooden box full of coins sitting on the counter in front of him, and started shuffling. He then asked me if I was sure I didn't have the right change. I said I was, so he shuffled a bit more, but soon gave up and exclaimed, "Oh, fuck it! Just give it to me next time!" First, I blamed it on his insobriety, but then I realised he might have actually had problems figuring out how much change he was supposed to give back. But the Gardai should get their numbers right, no?

I go up the steps once again. Beer cans, fizzy drink bottles and ice cream wrapping now litter both sides of the entrance to the beach. The chipper is on the main road looking out onto the sea. A few people queue outside of it. I get there quick. No vinegar, but lots of salt, please! I sit down on one of the benches across the street on a dune, the bag in my left hand, a plastic fork in my right hand. They're salty and nice!

I can feel my face burning with all the sunshine and wind that it endured during the day. It's a pleasant feeling.

***

Several minutes later, I'm on the train to Dublin. It gets packed when we pull into Skerries. A couple take the seats opposite me. She's gorgeous, but he's not so much. And he looks knackered and bored. She hugs him tight and holds him like that for ever. But it's only my second railway ride on this side of the country, so even though they're an interesting sight, I take my eyes off the couple and look outside the window. I want to take in as much as possible.

The sea looks wonderful under the orange glow of the early-evening sun. And it actually feels like I'm on holiday. And hey! Look! The beach in Balbriggan is now a quarter of what it was this morning! The tide is coming in! It all makes sense now – those boats in the sand and all that.

I get off at Connolly Station. My feet are pure sore. It's difficult to walk. Like after my first hurling session last month that lasted for well over two hours. I limp along the Eden Quay Boardwalk, slowly and carefully. It's full of junkies shouting and smelling as always. I should have taken a different route. But it gets quieter after O'Connell Bridge. It's mainly locals and tourists here chilling out on the benches. I walk past them towards the setting sun, and I think I'll get a four-pack of Carlsberg in my local Spar to wrap up the day nicely.

LOST AND IN NEED OF
TRANSLATION

Dora has done some translation and interpreting before, but it has mostly been in quite an informal context and in the area that she feels rather comfortable in – music. But now they call her from one of the translation agencies that she has recently applied for work with, and they ask her to rush to the National Maternity Hospital in Holles Street. They give her no more than half an hour to get there, but she accepts the job. She turned down one other offer earlier this morning, when it caught her in bed. She was still awfully drowsy and unable to gather her thoughts, but then she worried the agency might never call her again. And so she promised to herself that if they did call her, she would take the job no matter what. And they do now – forty minutes later – though they give her no information on the nature of the interpreting that she will be asked to do. She will get more details when she arrives at the hospital, they say.

She hails a taxi, as she does not even know where the hospital is. But on this particularly dark and rainy October morning a taxi would be necessary anyway. And while the driver skilfully manoeuvres their way through the dense rush-hour traffic on O'Connell Street, fighting against the hammer of rain attacking the windscreen, Dora wonders if she will be able to cope with what is about to be thrown at her – also in the literal sense, as she is rather on the sensitive side of things. If she sees a baby covered in blood and birth fluids, or if she slips on the placenta splashed out on the floor – let alone having to witness the cutting of the cord – she will most certainly faint. Hospitals have always made her cringe and sweat. Even the briefest glimpse of a syringe sends a terribly cold shiver down her spine. She therefore hopes no one will ask her to interpret while the client convulses with labour pain.

The nurse would go: "Push!"

Then Dora: "Nyomd!"

The patient would scream: "Nem tudom!!!"

And Dora: "I can't!!!"

On O'Connell Bridge, she looks up *pregnancy* in Wikipedia to make sure she is familiar with at least the most basic terminology. Strangely enough, the agency had not checked her language skills before they gave her the job. They had only asked for papers proving her language proficiency.

On her arrival at the hospital, Dora is surprised by how claustrophobic the place feels – it looks like a big, old townhouse adapted for use as a hospital. In one of its dark and narrow corridors she is met by a young midwife who immediately takes her to a grey-haired, all-wrinkled social worker whose name Dora does not manage to catch, but who seems to be taken aback by how young Dora is. As a result, the small office the social worker resides in fills with an unpleasant air of mistrust.

But Dora tries to behave as if she knew what she was doing. She listens to the instructions very carefully: the social worker wants to talk to a young Hungarian woman who has just become a mother, but who – unusually – never receives any visitors or phone calls. Therefore, the old lady wants to check if everything is fine, if the new mother has someone who will be able to help her with her new responsibilities once she leaves the hospital, and, consequently, if the baby will be provided with adequate care.

The midwife then takes Dora to a big ward in which beds are arranged in two rows – one to the left of the ward, and one to the right. Each bed is hidden from the world behind colourful curtains. On the bed behind the second curtain to the left, in her stained blue pyjamas sits Barbara. She looks like any other woman in the hospital – shagged out and dishevelled, but also relieved.

When Dora explains to Barbara why she has come to visit her, Barbara – even though she has no English whatsoever – seems slightly embarrassed that a stranger needs to assist her. The midwife smiles pleasantly and leaves the Hungarian ladies for a minute or two to let the ice-breaking continue.

Barbara becomes noticeably worried when Dora tells her that the social worker wants to meet her, and it does not make her feel any better when Dora clarifies that the meeting has only been arranged to ensure that everything is fine with Barbara – nothing to be anxious about. The young mother, however, gives an impression of someone who would prefer to be left alone. She seems rather uneducated and lost – like someone who has never experienced anything like this before. And Barbara indeed has not. It is her first child.

But Dora is nervous too, so she has no difficulty empathising with Barbara. She tries to make Barbara feel at ease, at the same time hiding her own insecurities behind a reassuring smile. She asks how Barbara feels and how the baby is. But before Barbara is able to answer, the nurse comes back and asks them to follow her to the social worker's office.

The social worker is now like a completely different person – all smiles and friendliness. She asks Barbara to take a seat in front of her, across the desk. Dora finds a spot beside Barbara – just behind her, slightly to her right. She tries to focus and remember all the rules of good interpreting: be invisible; note down the main points; talk calmly and clearly; translate only what is said – never add anything; do not get drawn into a conversation with any of the parties.

Barbara is asked, through Dora, if she feels fine, and – through Dora again – she confirms that she does. Then, the social worker asks where Barbara lives and who with. But Barbara cannot remember the exact address – she can only recall the postcode. She lives with her two sisters. Both sisters are married.

When Barbara is asked about the father of the child, she hangs her head down and becomes even more reluctant to answer the questions. She just says, quietly, that she does not know where the father is. In fact, she does not know who the father is, or so she claims. The social worker informs Barbara that the name of the father needs to be provided for the birth certificate, or else it will state *unknown*. Barbara confirms that she does not know the name, which brings a lump to Dora's throat, and which clearly upsets Barbara.

The social worker then asks Barbara if there is anything that the hospital staff could do for her, but the only thing Barbara wants is to know when she will be allowed to go home.

Before they leave the social worker's office, the old lady once again enquires if Barbara is sure she will be OK. And when Barbara nods, she is allowed to go back to her bed. Dora is dismissed too. She feels relieved that her first interpreting job went so smoothly, but deep down she also feels great sadness, wondering what will happen with Barbara. After all, the poor girl is in a foreign country without the language, uneducated, forgotten by everyone, and now with a baby. Dora is glad to see that at least the hospital staff do their best to provide her with the care she needs.

Although it still rains, Dora decides to walk. She has an umbrella, and she needs some fresh air and some solitude. The streets are busy with cars splashing water on the early-lunch crowds who graciously leap over the multitude of puddles forming at their feet, and who swirl their colourful umbrellas as if performing in some bizarre dance show. But Dora walks unaffected by all the swarm and bustle, lost in her thoughts and looking up at the massive, dripping wet and still juicy green trees which branch out over the fence of Merrion

Square Park. She breaths in the warm, early-autumn air and meditates on how the aura that surrounds her is now a perfect reflection of her feelings.

***

The next morning, Dora is asked to go to Beaumont Hospital. She enquires what type of interpreting she will need to do there, but the agent once again is not able to provide any additional information. Dora is only informed, in a rather brusque manner, that, in general, the company does not receive any details from the clients. This takes her by surprise, as it is simply against the most basic rules of good practice of interpreting, but she does get the message that if she wishes to continue working as an interpreter for this company, she will need to adapt.

In the hospital, a patient representative warns Dora that she will be translating at an intensive care unit for a young Hungarian lady who has got a tube inserted into a hole in her throat, and who is therefore unable to speak. Dora will need to read her lips. And because the patient is in a condition that might be difficult to look at, Dora is advised to stop interpreting and excuse herself whenever she feels like taking a break.

Dora is glad to hear that the staff are understanding, but she also realises how serious the situation must be if she gets warnings of that sort. And knowing all too well that she faints at the mere sight of blood and needles, she becomes seriously concerned that she might not be able to complete the assigned job. She shares these feelings with the representative, but the Irish lady only tries to calm her down, chanting like a mantra, "You'll be fine, love! You'll be fine!" She clearly does not understand. No one can ever understand how sensitive Dora is.

And the situation in the post-operative room is indeed serious: an accident has left a young woman unable to move her body from neck down. The doctor wants Dora to explain to the patient what has been done to improve her condition, as well as what steps will next be taken to bring her back to the state from before the accident.

As the doctor speaks, and as Dora translates, two nurses rush around the bed adjusting the drips hanging beside and over the bed, and giving the patient countless injections. And this is when Dora starts noticing a multitude of tiny, silvery spots before her, and in her ears a whistle that grows increasingly loud. But she waits too long. When she finally informs the hospital personnel that she needs to leave, it is already too late – the two nurses have to grab her by the arms and help her out of the room. In the corridor, she is made to sit with her legs up on a chair placed in front of her in order to restore blood flow to the brain. The nurses also help her remove the heavy jacket that, for some reason, she still has on. Then they serve her with a glass of cold water.

Knowing that she has a mission to complete, Dora comes round fast, though she is acutely embarrassed by how sensitive she is to the things that most people would not be affected by. But the hospital staff are very supportive, and when Dora finally brings herself to enter the room again, they all pick up from where they left off: the doctor enquires how the patient feels and if there is anything that she needs.

Dora finds it extremely challenging to understand what the Hungarian lady attempts to get across, her voice replaced by a wheeze of air let out through the tube stuck in her neck. There is no other way to communicate than through lip-reading. But this proves very difficult. In order to get at least the key words, Dora needs to go through the alphabet and have the patient nod once she arrives at the right letter. As time consuming and exhausting as it is, it does allow Dora to eventually put the letters together into words.

The patient is mainly interested in what is happening with her children. Large tears start flowing down her cheeks when she asks about them. The nurses later explain to Dora that the children – a boy and a girl, 7 and 5 respectively – came to the hospital accompanied by their father – the patient's husband – shortly after the patient had been admitted, but since then – for the last five days – there has been no contact with them. And when Dora is asked to call the mobile number provided by the husband, the man on the other end of the line claims he does not know the lady in question. He says the hospital must have been given a wrong number.

After straining her hearing and sight for ninety minutes, at the same time doing her best not to faint again, Dora is sincerely thanked by the hospital staff and then let go. She leaves the place numbed with the realisation of how difficult life can be for some people, how fragile the human body is, and how helpless one can become when caught in the wrong place at the wrong time. Paralysed from neck down and thus not being able to do anything while someone clearly tries to keep her children away from her – it can hardly get any worse, Dora thinks. She feels guilty she cannot do more to help. She hopes the hospital will look into the issue, or will at least be able to assist the patient with contacting the relevant authorities.

Although she still feels somewhat dizzy, Dora deliberately takes a bus back into town, not a taxi. She is in no hurry to get back home. She would rather stay with her face glued to the bus window, staring at the amazing oaks that line up Swords Road and Upper Drumcondra Road, and which now start dropping leaves. She doubts she will ever see the paralysed woman again. She is sure the hospital will request a different interpreter next time – someone who will be solving problems, not creating them.

***

Over the following three weeks, Dora is sent to a number of different institutions: Cloverhill Prison, where she interprets for a middle-aged, bearded man who seems unpredictable and violent, who left Hungary while awaiting trial, and who might not have been hunted down by the Guards had he not been spotted lifting rubbish bags from the boot of his car and chucking them into a supermarket's skip; a solicitor's office in the Heineken building, where a man claims to have been unfairly fired; the Neurology Department of Children's University Hospital in Temple Street, where Dora helps the doctor communicate with a seven-year-old girl who was in a short coma following a fall and a head bump, and who, as a result, seemed to suffer some memory loss; and a psychologist's office in the Greystones Health Centre, where a woman finds her maternal responsibilities difficult to cope with.

Dora is also sent to the St. Aloysius Ward in Mater Hospital – the Acute Mental Health Unit. There, after a long wait, she meets a psychiatrist – a young and gracious, yet rather serious and tired-looking Irish lady with white skin, a ginger ponytail, and an attractive sprinkling of freckles all over her face and neck – who explains that Dora will be interpreting between her and a patient who is schizophrenic, or who, she stresses, just pretends to be. And the conversation the doctor wants to conduct with the patient is supposed to discover just that: whether the patient is genuinely sick or simply faking it.

This brief outline of the situation ends when an unshaven, all tousled forty-something with a sad face and a head hung low shuffles in led by a nurse, a monstrous beer gut flapping over the top of his filthy pyjama trousers. Dora introduces herself and proceeds to explain what she is going to do, but Janos seems to already know everything. He says there was another interpreter, or two, assisting him before Dora. She knows nothing about it, but – out of professionalism – she pretends she has indeed been informed.

In response to the psychiatrist's questions, Janos says he does not feel well – he is weak and he lives in constant fear. And he hears voices.

"How many voices?" the doctor investigates.

"A few different voices," Janos says, looking down at his feet.

"What do they say?" the doctor asks.

"They…" Janos hesitates. "They tell me to… tell me to kill myself."

When Dora translates that very last sentence, she lets out a quiet smirk. Janos does not seem to notice, but the doctor does. And Dora is now overcome with embarrassment, acutely aware of the fact that what she has just done was entirely inappropriate and highly unprofessional.

The psychiatrist then enquires if the voices say anything else. Janos assures her that they do not. How often does he hear them? He hears them all the time. And now Dora starts pitying Janos, the kid from The Sixth Sense springs to mind:

I see dead people.
I see them all the time.
They're everywhere!

The doctor then allows Janos to ask questions, but Janos does not seem to have any. He only informs the psychiatrist that whatever happens, he does not agree to ECT.

At this point, Dora still does not know that ECT stands for electroconvulsive therapy, but the context – and even more so Janos's horror-ridden yet determined face – leaves no doubt as to how serious the thing must be.

The doctor assures Janos that the hospital has no plans to perform ECT on him, but Janos repeats what he has just said, as if he has never said it before, and as if the doctor has not just confirmed there would be no ECT – or as if he wanted to emphasise that he knows his rights perfectly well and that without his consent the hospital can do nothing.

Janos then becomes calmer and enquires how much longer he will be kept in hospital. And a week or two does not seem to surprise him. He understands that the doctor needs that time to establish an accurate diagnosis.

Having his question answered, Janos stuns Dora by directing his next question at her. He asks for a cigarette. And when she says she does not smoke, he asks her again. He does not believe her. His hands shake and he looks nervous. He is desperate. And he asks Dora not to translate that part. But the doctor wants to know what Janos said, so Dora feels obliged to explain.

Neither the doctor nor the nurse appear surprised, though, when they hear what he wants. He apparently keeps bugging everyone for cigarettes. And he does not give up so easily – before he is led out of the doctor's office, he begs

Dora to bring him a few cigs next time around. He promises to give her the money back. The doctor explains, however, that Janos will not give her the money back, as he simply does not have any. As far as she knows, he is flat broke. Skint. But Dora does not worry about the money. She has already decided that she will bring him a pack if only the agency asks her to interpret for Janos again.

***

The agency asks her two days later, so on her way to the hospital she pops into a newsagent's to get the smokes. And it feels very strange. The last time she bought cigarettes must have been thirteen or fourteen years ago, when she was experimenting with smoking – as most kids do, innocently. But now she cannot remember any of the brands. She needs to ask the assistant what cigarettes they sell. And when she hears *Camels*, which her old man used to smoke, and which almost killed him, she goes for them. They are bloody expensive, she notices. But she also buys a lighter – just in case the poor chap does not have one either.

In the hospital, she finds out that this time she has only been asked for a short consultation. The doctor is late again, so Dora makes herself comfortable in a small armchair in the corridor. Janos spots her there and takes a seat across a small coffee table from her, his jumper now even dirtier than last time.

He asks if she has a fag. She says she does not, that she is not allowed to give him any. She does not want to show him the Camels just yet, as she is not sure how he will react. She prefers to wait until the consultation is over. And she also wants to confirm with the nurse that the hospital has nothing against her bringing him gifts.

Janos tells Dora where exactly he is from in Hungary, as well as how long he has been in Ireland. Then, he asks where Dora is from. She answers him, and then she just stares at his heavy, grizzled stubble. She does not want to ask him any questions. She feels it would be inappropriate. But Janos tells her a bit about himself anyway. And there is nothing from his past that stands out for Dora – it is his future that looks bleak. He does not know what he is going to do when they finally let him out of hospital.

For some reason, though, Janos seems more relaxed today. He even starts joking. That, in turn, makes Dora lighten up – to the point that she allows herself to ask him about what she has had on her mind since her first visit to the St. Aloysius Ward: if he really hears the voices, or if he only puts it on.

Janos's answer takes Dora by surprise. He actually looks offended. He raises his voice and makes it clear that he would never lie – not in a hospital. He says it is not a place for making jokes. Then he just cuts it out, his face red and his eyes bulging. But he does not leave. He remains in his seat.

Dora apologises sincerely, and they just keep sitting beside each other in awkward silence, waiting for the doctor, who now cannot arrive soon enough. But Dora's intuition does not want to give her a break. She feels Janos is not honest with her. She reckons he simply does not trust her enough to tell her the truth. He might even suspect her of being a spy. He might think that she has been specifically asked by the doctor to put that question to him.

During the consultation, the doctor learns that the voices are still there, but now they are not there all the time – they come and go. The doctor tells him that he will most probably soon be released home. He nods, but he does not look happier.

After the consultation, when Janos is already gone, Dora tells the doctor and the nurse about the cigarettes. Both ladies praise her for her good heart, and then the nurse shows her to Janos's bed. And the way Janos reacts when he catches sight of that lousy pack of Camels will stay in Dora's heart forever. She has never seen anyone so happy.

Janos thanks her so many times that she starts feeling embarrassed. And he shakes her hand so hard that she starts feeling uncomfortable. And the tears that brim in his eyes bring tears into hers.

***

A few days later, Dora is requested back to the St. Aloysius Ward. This time, though, it all feels strange from the very first minute – she needs to ring the intercom to be let in, whereas normally the door is not locked. One of the nurses explains, without any inhibitions, that the reason behind those extra precautions is that Janos tried to hang himself on his leather belt the previous night. Fortunately, he did not succeed. Now he is on a suicide watch.

Dora and Janos meet in the same armchairs where they spoke last time. But now they are accompanied by a nurse. She is on him twenty-four seven. The three of them wait for the doctor to arrive.

To Dora's surprise, Janos is in a relatively good mood – the best she has actually ever seen him in. They talk in Hungarian. The nurse cannot understand them.

"You see," he snorts, "she follows me everywhere, including the bathroom! But look at her! Look! If only she were that tiny bit more attractive!" They both burst out laughing, even though Dora finds it slightly offensive.

Several minutes later, in the doctor's office, the scenario is replayed once again: the same questions – similar responses. But this time, the doctor confirms that the hospital has taken action to ensure Janos will have a place to stay in and someone to look after him when he gets out.

When Janos leaves the doctor's office – as slowly as ever, and as ever shuffling his heavy feet clad in a pair of stained, beige slippers – it is the last time Dora sees him. She will never again be asked by the agency to assist Janos, but she will often wonder how he is – or if he is at all.

HER & ME

Last night, I dreamt about an ideal woman. I don't know who she was, nor do I remember what she looked like, but I know she was perfect. Then, I dreamt about flying.

Now, leaning against the wooden railings on the faintly-lit porch of my holiday cabin by the Baltic, a drink in hand, I listen to the midnight silence and look out into the darkness. It's late September and almost all holidaymakers have already deserted the place. Even the insects in that waist-tall grass surrounding the cabin have stopped conversing their usual way. And the mysterious creature that

139

kept scratching under the floor of the cabin has now gone too.

A thick blanket of fog hangs low over the small tobacco field to my left. Behind it, separated only by a narrow strip of forest, the sea sleeps peacefully. To my right, far in the distance, a dim light signals rare human presence in one of the several shadow-like houses seated on the side of a small hill. And here, right beside me, a night bird passes by making a soft, swooshing sound. And I just wonder if finding a perfect girl is as impossible as flying.

I thought it wouldn't be, because it hadn't been really. I did have it at one point. She was my soul mate. But then I gave it all away. And what ensued was pure decadence.

BOUTIQUE

BLOND

JACKET

LEGS

GLASSES

GLANCE

CLOSENESS

TRUST

CARE

FUN

LOVE

she said she did. But I didn't say anything. Didn't know what to say. Just smiled. I couldn't lie. Then she said it again, and then again one more time (third time lucky?). But I could only hug her.

I did fall for her, though, earlier – at the very beginning. She was full of child-like energy. And she had unpierced ears. And she was so affectionate! So crazy! We made love in a car in a church yard in some small town nearby Dundalk (or was it Newry?) on our way to the Giant's Causeway, and then again by Lough Neigh; and I got her off on a plane from Paris, and on the bed that she shared with her sister and where we were later caught. And maybe it was just to run away from that sister that she wanted to move in with me. But how?! The thoughts behind those big, gorgeous eyes, the ideals, the whole mindset – everything! – was so different from mine! We couldn't communicate once the curtains had been drawn back. The break-up was inevitable.

We missed each other, though, and we often got back together – but only like animals: to satisfy our

LUST

ON-LINE

DINNER

DRINKS

JUICE

loads of it! Her constant turning from side to side woke me up the next morning. It was flowing from her, gluing her ginger curls together and wetting her thighs – and not letting her sleep. We met one more time about a month later to do it all again.

The next girl liked the Stones and yoga, but was a bit of a hipster (i.e. doing certain things because they are cool and not necessarily because doing them gives the doer satisfaction, and not doing certain things because they are not cool, though they might be the most amazing things to do ever). And the reek from her private parts! Simply unbearable. I could smell it through her tights. And I'm not exaggerating! Pheromones it certainly wasn't. I just couldn't! I liked her, though, for some reason, and I was willing to try to make it work out, or at least shag her properly, but – alas! – she broke up with me.

She worked for Google, and so did the next one. The fact that I knew a lot of people from outside of the Google ghetto (a popular name for the area around Barrow Street) impressed that next one big time. She didn't like her job, and she hated being surrounded by her colleagues, and generally by people who talked about nothing but work. She was trying to find her way out of there, or so she claimed.

Some time later, we bumped into each other. She'd had a child with someone from the office (a baby rocking in a cradle wearing one of those stupid Google caps and a Google T-shirt?). The irony of life! But I genuinely hope she's now happier than she used to be.

NIGHTCLUB

SAMHAIN

MADNESS

STRANGER

INTOXICATION

to the point where on my way back from the bar I could no longer remember what she looked like or where we'd parted. I had to stand in the middle of that big club, surrounded by whirling skeletons and flashing stroboscopes, and wait, hoping she would find me. And she did. We then started making out in the crowd, kissing and rubbing against each other, and as she slid under my Grim Reaper robe, I again found myself standing there on my own, with a scythe in one hand and a coke and Jack in the other. This time, however, I didn't feel lonely. When she reappeared, I went to get another drink, but in that haze of alcoholic stupor I was doomed to get lost once again. And this time I got lost for good. Insert a sad face here.

The following night, though, I met someone else – a professional dancer. And we had a great time together, despite the fact that I'm a terrible dancer. But I gave it all I had, and that must have been appreciated, because we slithered like snakes all night, right until closing time. And only then, when the music had gone silent, and the terribly colourful disco lights had been switched off, did she announce that she had to return to her husband. She wanted to keep in touch, though. But it wasn't the same the second time around.

The night at the Theatre@36 in Teachers' Club in Parnell Square, a few months later, ended up being similarly awkward. I'd gone alone, for I don't mind going alone (in fact, only that day in the morning did I discover it was the last chance to see the play – and I'd been meaning to see it for some time – so I didn't even bother to ask if anyone would be interested in joining me at such a short notice), but I'd made one of the books I'd been reading be my companion.

And as I was reading during the interval, sipping Smithwick's at one of the tall stools lined up neatly beside the mirror-covered wall of the bar, minding my own business, a girl in a red dress and a matching lipstick sat two stools away from me. A mane of long, crow-black, wavy hair fell heavily on her right shoulder, one lock nearly plunging into the wine that she was holding close to her cleavage. Her left hand opened a programme. And I noticed all that in one quick glance. I wasn't staring.

Apart from me, she was probably the only person there who'd come alone, and it must have made her feel slightly uncomfortable, because she took the very first opportunity, which was the announcement of the end of the interval, to part her sensuous lips and chat me up. She thought the interval had been cut short and she seemed unhappy with the fact that she wouldn't be able to finish her wine. We then exchanged a few pleasantries and headed back to the auditorium.

After the play, as I was directing myself from the bathroom towards the exit doors of the bar, I spotted her again. She was finishing her wine at one of the small tables in the middle of the bar. She'd wisely left the glass covered with a beer mat. I hadn't done that with my pint, so it was now gone. I smiled and asked if she'd enjoyed the play. She nodded and offered a seat. Unbuttoning my jacket, I asked if she was okay for wine. She thanked and said she'd already had enough. And as she proceeded to share her opinion about the show, and as I started to contemplate whether to get another drink for myself or better suggest going somewhere else for a couple, her boyfriend arrived. It occurred he was one of the supporting actors in the play. And when she told him that we'd just met, he can't have been taken aback much less than I was.

I left hastily, laughing to myself all the way down the stairs and out onto the street. I stood there for a moment and started counting in order to bring my heart rate down:

ONE

TWO

THREE

Yes, three, but not all at once – alternately. Like this: Friday – Korean night, Saturday – Czech night, Sunday – Dominican Republic night. Actually, with the Dominican one it had to wait until Monday morning, because by Sunday night I'd been so wrecked that I almost nodded off over the soup that she'd made for me. Cuddling up had to suffice that night. And it did wonderfully, for sleeping on a woman's breasts is the best way to sleep, her black skin being the softest I'd ever caressed, and her kiss more sensuous than any other kiss that had ever been planted on me.

Sure, I knew it was all wrong, but somehow one thing had led to another and it just ended up like that. It definitely hadn't been planned. But they were all so nice! And that winter was so cold! And why are there only twenty-four hours in a day?!

Seriously, though, of course it couldn't last long, nor was it supposed to. It would soon start getting confusing. I mean, the names never got confused, but getting some basic facts wrong here and there was unavoidable, not to mention the need to explain things like scratches on the back, the odd love bite, or a hair of a different colour on the pillow. But even if they catch you red-handed, the old adage goes, say it's not your hand!

I enjoyed that time, I have to be honest, but I also felt utterly ashamed of myself – or at least a bit – especially knowing that one of them had been cheated on and lied to on numerous occasions before. I didn't want to be another prick who'd hurt her. I didn't want to hurt any of them. Therefore, I soon decided it would be best to let all of them go. Life, though, as life often does, had other plans. But that is, I guess, a story for another book.

INTELLECT

CHARM

CONFIDENCE

WIT

PASSION

INQUISITIVENESS

COMMITMENT

she wanted to have spelled out in capital letters. She wanted more and more, but how could I have given it to her if I knew she wasn't the one, that she was there only to satisfy that primal need for physical closeness? And so I had to search through the vast reservoir of language for words that would allow talking about feelings in a way that wouldn't give her false promises, yet also in a way that would keep her coming back.

She was a psychologist. A short, sensuously curvy, baby-faced and graced with long blond hair psychologist. Bursting with sexual desire. When she was alone, she'd finger herself and record it. And then she'd watch it. And she was equally much fun to talk to. We spent many a night arguing about stuff, but we argued in a manner that was mutually respectful, quite insightful and always enlightening. It was less fun, though, when she started overanalysing things and trying to fix what wasn't broken. Interesting to observe, because she'd always say that the field of psychology was saturated with creeps and losers who were barely able to figure out their own lives, but who would then put on a serious face at nine in the morning and pretend to know how to help other people, yet it struck me that she had similar issues.

SEXESEXESEXESEXESEXESEXESEXESEXESEXESE
XESEXESEXESEXESEXESEXESEXESEXESEXESEXE

SEXESEXESEXESEXESEXESEXESEXESEXESEXSEX
ESEXESEXESEXESEXESEXESEXESEXESEXESEXES
EXESEXESEXESEXESEXESEXESEXESEXESEXESEX
ESEXESEXESEXESEXESEXESEXESEXESEXESEXES
EXESEXESEXESEXESEXESEXESEXESEXESEXESEX
ESEXESEXESEXESEXESEXESEXESEXESEXESEXES
EXESEXESEXESEXESEXESEXESEXESEXESEXESEX
ESEXESEXESEXESEXESEXESEXESEXESEXESEXES
EXESEXESEXESEXESEXESEXESEXESEXESEXESEX
ESEXESEXESEXESEXESEXESEXESEXESEXESEXES
EXESEXESEXESEXESEXESEXESEXESEXESEXESEX
ESEXESEXESEXESEXESEXESEXESEXESEXESEXES
EXESEXESEXESEXESEXESEXESEXESEXESEXESEX
ESEXESEXESEXESEXESEXESEXESEXESEXESEXES
EXESEXESEXESEXESEXESEXESEXESEXESEXESEX
ESEXESEXESEXESEXESEXESEXESEXESEXESEXES
EXESEXESEXESEXESEXESEXESEXESEXESEXESEX
ESEXESEXESEXESEXESEXESEXESEXESEXESEXES
EXESEXESEXESEXESEXESEXESEXESEXESEXESEX
ESEXESEXESEXESEXESEXESEXESEXESEXESEXES
EXESEXESEXESEXESEXESEXESEXESEXESEXESEX
ESEXESEXESEXESEXESEXESEXESEXESEXESEXES
EXESEXESEXESEXESEXESEXESEXESEXESEXESEX

151

SEXESEXEXESEXEXESEXEXESEXEXESEXEXESEXEXESEXEXESEXSEX
ESEXESEXEXESEXEXESEXEXESEXEXESEXEXESEXEXESEXEXESEXES
EXESEXEXESEXEXESEXEXESEXEXESEXEXESEXEXESEXEXESEXEXESEX
ESEXESEXEXESEXEXESEXEXESEXEXESEXEXESEXEXESEXEXESEXES
EXESEXEXESEXEXESEXEXESEXEXESEXEXESEXEXESEXEXESEXEXESEX
ESEXESEXEXESEXEXESEXEXESEXEXESEXEXESEXEXESEXEXESEXES
EXESEXEXESEXEXESEXEXESEXEXESEXEXESEXEXESEXEXESEXEXESEX
ESEXESEXEXESEXEXESEXEXESEXEXESEXEXESEXEXESEXEXESEXES
EXESEXEXESEXEXESEXEXESEXEXESEXEXESEXEXESEXEXESEXEXESEX
ESEXESEXEXESEXEXESEXEXESEXEXESEXEXESEXEXESEXEXESEXES
EXESEXEXESEXEXESEXEXESEXEXESEXEXESEXEXESEXEXESEXEXESEX
ESEXESEXEXESEXEXESEXEXESEXEXESEXEXESEXEXESEXEXESEXES
EXESEXEXESEXEXESEXEXESEXEXESEXEXESEXEXESEXEXESEXEXESEX
ESEXESEXEXESEXEXESEXEXESEXEXESEXEXESEXEXESEXEXESEXES
EXESEXEXESEXEXESEXEXESEXEXESEXEXESEXEXESEXEXESEXEXESEX
ESEXESEXEXESEXEXESEXEXESEXEXESEXEXESEXEXESEXEXESEXES
EXESEXEXESEXEXESEXEXESEXEXESEXEXESEXEXESEXEXESEXEXESEX
ESEXESEXEXESEXEXESEXEXESEXEXESEXEXESEXEXESEXEXESEXES
EXESEXEXESEXEXESEXEXESEXEXESEXEXESEXEXESEXEXESEXEXESEX
ESEXESEXEXESEXEXESEXEXESEXEXESEXEXESEXEXESEXEXESEXES
EXESEXEXESEXEXESEXEXESEXEXESEXEXESEXEXESEXEXESEXEXESEX
ESEXESEXEXESEXEXESEXEXESEXEXESEXEXESEXEXESEXEXESEXES
EXESEXEXESEXEXESEXEXESEXEXESEXEXESEXEXESEXEXESEXEXESEX

Surrounded by an aura of otherworldliness and myth, the concept of nymphomania has always been somewhat interesting to me. Every man is believed to fantasise about it, but once encountered in real life, it actually seems to be a phenomenon which one should rather be wary of. I myself thought I'd had one or two experiences with genuine hypersexuality, but the Latvian girl I met through work proved I knew nothing.

She was interested in theatre, so one day we decided to see something together. And it all began then.

She was not only sexually hyperactive but also generally hypersensitive. A simple touch would trigger an almost exaggerated response. She'd orgasm multiple times, and rather easily, and so intensively that she'd completely lose control over her body. And she always asked for more.

And she introduced me to bondage. She wanted to be tied up and beaten. And if a girl wants something, she gets it no matter how odd that thing might seem. Or does she?

Although it initially made me laugh, I enjoyed blindfolding her, taping her mouth and flagellating her luscious bottom and those tiny, sexy feet. I'd also viciously bite at her sides and thighs. But apart from spanking her buttocks, I'd have never hit her with a bare hand. It would have felt wrong. I sourced some gear from a sex shop.

Apart from S&M, she also introduced me to swallowing. I was surprised, as I'd always seen it as something rather degrading and repulsive, imposed on women by men who looked for abnormal ways to satisfy their sick desires (and, who knows, she too might have been encouraged to do it by one of her exes), but with me it was her who insisted on it. Each time I'd pull out or force her head away, she'd slag me off for, as she put it, being wasteful. And she said it tasted really good, even though she was a vegan.

She once also wanted me to spit in her mouth, but that I refused to do.

HIGHER!

HIGHER!

The tall, spectacled and fiercely intelligent film critic introduced me to anal sex. During our first night, when we were doing it doggy style, at one point she started chanting *Higher! Higher!* I thought she wanted me to enter her at a different angle, and so I tried, but later, while engaging in pillow talk, when I asked her what she liked, she fired without hesitation that she loved anal sex. And it suddenly became clear what that *Higher!* had meant.

She wasn't very impressed when I replied that I'd never tried it, and that I'd never really wanted to try. One of my ex-girlfriends had once or twice dropped a hint that if I fancied trying, she'd be up for it. She said that her previous boyfriend had asked her for anal sex, so she hadn't agreed. But if he hadn't asked, she said, she would have done it with him no problem. The thing was, however, I didn't feel like doing it at all. A mere thought of it made my brown eye sore. And it wouldn't have been me who'd have had a few inches of wood shovelled up in there, would it?!

But the film critic said she loved it, so I decided to learn the ropes. I looked up some video tutorials on the net, and after two hours I felt I was ready for our second date. And it went pretty smoothly, though I have to admit I didn't feel that much of a difference in there. Yes, it was indeed a bit tighter, but it wasn't as tight as one could be led to believe. That tightness can easily be felt with a finger, but a proper hard-on is, I think, simply too hard to sense it.

I quickly got hooked on it, and I initiated my subsequent girlfriend. As much as it surprised her, she enjoyed the whole novelty of it. She also liked spanking, bondage and handcuffing.

She, in turn, introduced me to pissing. But I didn't like it. The state of the bed! Imagine! We'd often have to make love in the bath.

And we had amazing chemistry, bar the pissing part. She didn't speak much English. And I didn't speak any Spanish (*Salud!*). My dad wanted to know how we talked then, but that was the whole point – we didn't talk much. It was great not to have to discuss a movie that we'd just seen, or books that we were reading. We just sucked each other. And who knows, maybe that was the reason why it lasted so long. But then again, her English had to improve sooner or later.

CANDLES

FLOWERS

DILDO

SATIATION

DEBAUCHERY

PAGEANTRY

INADEQUACY

FILTH

OFFICE

INFATUATION

LONGING

ESCORT

DUBLIN

LIMERICK

CORK

WARSAW

EMBARRASSMENT

REFUSAL

SPUNK

IN

THE

EYE

LAUGHTER

FREEDOM

SOLITUDE

APATHY

DISINTEREST

INDIFFERENCE

DISAPPOINTMENT

And so I keep searching, although Baudelaire seems to be whispering in my ear that I might as well be sunk up to the knee in the grave of the ideal. But I like to think that the ideal is actually out there alive and in good health. And I hope I'll find it one day – or it'll find me. Because I'm worth it!

TO BE ON TIME

For my parents

It had never been his dream to work for a corporation, yet there he was, sitting in that spacious, shining lobby of the European headquarters of the biggest search engine in the world, opposite a long reception desk, patiently waiting for the manager of his new team to collect him and introduce him to his colleagues.

No, that actually is not entirely true: Damian had applied for a job with a big, international company a few years before – with Tesco. Back then, they were recruiting in Krakow for management positions in their UK superstores, and the Polish lad was just out of university, right after defending his MA thesis in linguistics, but he had also already managed to gain some managerial experience while being in charge of a language school – a job that he had given up in order to concentrate on finishing his thesis and preparing for the final exams.

And so, even though Damian was totally aware that at the age of twenty-four he was way too young for the Tesco job, he decided to go for it full on. After all, hadn't he also been too young for the head of school position? Besides, he thought any excuse to pay Krakow yet another visit was good enough.

***

Damian got through the first stages of the recruitment process, which included a phone screening, two face-to-face interviews, a language test and an aptitude tests, but he failed in the last round – role-play tasks.

When he later analysed what had happened during those role-play tasks, whether he had done anything wrong, he started suspecting that there had been an insider in the group, a rat – the young, petite, yet very self-confident blonde who acted somewhat awkwardly. It would have made perfect sense for the HR team to place a spy among the candidates in order to eavesdrop on their real attitudes towards the job, and on their opinions about the company. And Damian did say one or two things too many while talking to the other candidates during the breaks between the tasks.

If he had got the job, he wouldn't have stayed with Tesco for very long anyway, though. It was just supposed to be an easy way onto the islands – nothing more. Damian wanted to spend some time abroad, chilling out and improving his language skills in the natural environment, but he didn't have any money saved, so he thought finding a job while he was still in Poland, instead of going abroad without anything set up and then risk running out of funds, was the right way of going about things. In the UK, Damian thought, he would leave the company as soon as he collected the first couple of payslips.

But he didn't get the job. Not getting it didn't stop him going ahead with his plan, though. He was hell bent on leaving somewhere, so over the next few of weeks he looked through his considerable collection of CDs, placed the ones he didn't like very much on Allegro (Polish eBay), and collected over 3000 PLN (around 750 euros) from their sales. That – plus the few bob that he had in his bank account – added up to around 1200 euros. He felt it wasn't bad for the start. And on top of that, he won a return ticket with SkyEurope in a text message competition that he had found in one of the weekly magazines on his train journey back home from Krakow, after the Tesco interviews. He could travel free of charge, bar the airport taxes, wherever and whenever he wanted in Europe.

Damian also knew that his parents would help him out if he ran into trouble. They always made sure to stress that they were there for him if he needed anything. But financial help was the last thing he wanted to ask them for. He had been living independently for quite some time, and he was determined to keep it that way.

Neither did he consider contacting any of his friends based in the UK. He had never really liked imposing himself on others. Even more importantly, though, he wanted a proper adventure. And because there were no friends in Ireland that he knew of, it seemed to be the right place to hit.

There were, however, a good few of his fellow compatriots living on the Emerald Isle, and the rumour had it that they had found employment there no problem. If they had managed, Damian thought, he would be fine too. And he only wanted a simple job – nothing particularly demanding. He had had enough of ten- or twelve-hour work days, and studying for his MA on top of that. And the job abroad wasn't supposed to be for a long time either – a few months max.

In short, Damian wanted a break, wanted to take it easy, do some travelling, and read the books he hadn't been able to read due to his enormous workload. Only after that, with his batteries recharged, he would go back to university to do his PhD.

***

Once the country had been chosen, the question as to which city to invade didn't need to be asked. It had to be Dublin – a city that he had heard about numerous times from Mr Joyce and Mr Lynott, and for whose more up-to-date information he approached Ms Google. And he instantly loved the fact that Dublin didn't appear to be a huge metropolis, and that the average summer temperature there wasn't too high. And that the average winter temperature wasn't too low. And also that there was a river running right through the city, and that the city was on the coast. It seemed he liked everything about it.

A one-way flight booking confirmation soon landed in his e-mail. Then, Booking.com recommended something cheap for the first week. He hoped one week would be enough to get a job and find proper accommodation. The money he had organised would pay the first two weeks' rent, and after that he would get his wages. That was the plan.

The place which he booked was in one of the student accommodation buildings in University College Dublin. It was relatively cheap: 30 euros a night in a single room, bathroom shared with three other rooms. The location was not too bad either, and because it was a university campus, it was well-served by public transport.

Soon afterwards, Damian started looking for a job on Jobs.ie, as well as in some Polish newspapers which, at that time, also included ads from abroad. He sent out several CVs, and it didn't take long for a few people to express their interest in him. But they all wanted to be contacted again only after Damian's arrival in Dublin.

***

He landed on the morning of July 3, 2007. The cool breeze that brushed his face on his way down the airstairs was the first thing he noticed, followed by the white clouds that sped above him and that let the bright summer sun out only sporadically, and only for a few seconds. Damian loved it. Back at home it was scorching.

He had been meaning to read about Ireland – and particularly about Dublin – in a tourist guide that he had been given as a good-luck gift before he left, but he couldn't concentrate on the plane. The mounting excitement wouldn't let him. When the plane landed, though, he knew what to do: he got himself an Irish sim card, and then he found a coach that would take him to UCD.

The coach was packed, but Damian somehow managed to secure a window seat, and as they were leaving the airport, he just couldn't help but look up at the sky and marvel at how rapidly it was changing. Then, when they got closer to town, he gazed with childlike anxiety at the elegant terraced houses in the upper part of Drumcondra, and at the colourful pubs along Dorset Street. Later: the Spire, which he had seen on the Internet, and which he now thought looked amazing in its modern simplicity, towering over the old city and reflecting the sun.

Damian jumped off the bus beside the UCD campus, but it took him an hour to find the right building, his hand luggage and the main bag a crippling burden. And because it was still too early to check in, he left the bag and caught a bus back into town. He had his CVs stuck into plastic folders, waiting patiently somewhere between a city map and a laptop for their chance to impress prospective employers, but he didn't want to start distributing them just yet. He first wanted to get to know the city.

***

All that wandering around alone and getting lost in the narrow streets of Dublin made Damian feel as free as ever.

In the evening, he chatted to the girls who he shared the accommodation with, enjoying the fact that he was being exposed to so many different accents and cultures: there was a Canadian, a Norwegian, and an Irish girl from County Carlow.

Later in the night, he made sure to email those few people who had already contacted him regarding work to let them know he was already in Dublin.

The next morning, putting on the suit that he had brought with him, Damian went into town and left his CV with two recruitment agencies. But a few minutes spent in their offices were enough for him to realise that relying on agencies of that sort would be a waste of time. With CVs piled up on every desk and in every corner, and just pure chaos all around, they seemed unlikely to be able to sort him out.

Fortunately, though, when Damian sat in a café for lunch, he saw he had received an email from the manager of a city centre car rental shop, Shane, who wanted to interview him the following day. And no sooner had he finished reading that email than his mobile rang. It was the manager of a boutique hotel that Damian had emailed the previous night. The hotel, as Damian later found out, was around the corner from the café he was sitting in. The hotel manager, too, wanted to interview him the following day.

Damian met the rent-a-car manager first. They had a quick chat over the counter, but Shane spoke fast and with a strong Dublin accent, so Damian could barely understand him. He must have nonetheless made a good impression on the short Irishman, for the next morning he was offered the post of a car rental agent. And it was just as well, because the interview for the position of a night-shift manager in the hotel had not gone that smoothly. Both Damian and the manager of the hotel seemed to have a pleasant conversation, but from the very first minute it was obvious that Damian had no idea whatsoever about running a hotel – nor did he have any interest in learning the ropes. He had clearly done no research before coming to the interview, and the best thing he could do was to laugh away at the silly answers he was throwing at that bulky gentleman in a neat suit sitting in front of him in a tiny office in the vaults of the hotel.

***

Damian stayed with the car rental place for almost a year. It was much longer than he had initially intended, but he enjoyed the freedom it gave him: eight-hour work days, including an hour for lunch, flexibility in choosing his days off, low car rental rates for the staff, and a fairly relaxed atmosphere in the workplace. And Shane, even though he hated punters – all of them being an unnecessary bother for him – occurred to be a rather cool guy, always making sure to treat his staff in the fairest possible way.

The pay, however, was not great (the minimum wage plus a five-percent commission), so after a few months of living on the breadline, Damian started giving private English lessons to other Polish people based in Dublin. And there happened to be quite some interest in his services, and it paid well, so he quickly managed to increase his standard of living to a level that he was happy with.

Enjoying the one-to-one tuition, and regaining his enthusiasm for teaching, Damian soon applied for evening work with a language school in Blanchardstown. The management were renting some rooms in one of the community centres there.

On the day of the interview, however, Damian didn't seem too concerned with the whole thing. With as little as half an hour to go before the scheduled meeting, he was still sitting on his bed in Fairview with a map spread in front of him, trying to find the best way to get to that community centre.

When he finally took off, he realised he had left the map at home. And as he wasn't very fond of sat-nav, he didn't have one in the car. His phone didn't have one either. But because it was already getting extremely late, he decided against turning back to get the map. He hoped he would be able to find the place without it. In case of any problems, he would stop and ask someone for directions. No big deal, he thought.

He was actually far more concerned about the car that he was driving – a brand new, red as red could be Audi A3 sport – the only car left that day in the car rental place, and therefore the only one that he had been able to take. It fitted into the image of a responsible English teacher like a fist fits into a nose.

When driving through Phibsborough towards the N3, Damian received a call from Rob – one of the two managers of the school – double checking if Damian remembered about the meeting. Damian said he did, but he mentioned nothing about running late. In fact, for some reason he said he would be with Rob shortly. Fortunately, as it was already after 8 p.m., the traffic had eased off.

Speeding recklessly, Damian must have taken a wrong turn into Blanchardstown, since nothing really looked there like it had on the road map at home. It was all too vast and each street resembled another with those typical suburban detached and semi-detached houses lined up on both sides, with lawns, little driveways and joggers running by.

Driving around for several minutes, Damian decided to ask someone for help. As luck would have it, though, no one seemed to be aware of any community centre in that area. Growing anxious, Damian decided to call Rob and explain he had got lost. The school manager very patiently gave him all the instructions that he needed to find his way around, but the Polish lad can't have listened carefully, because he still couldn't find it. He kept driving in circles for the next hour or so, receiving two calls from the increasingly irritated manager, as well as troubling a few passers-by for directions. And if it hadn't been for the good-hearted taxi driver, Damian would have never found the place.

When he finally drove into the car park in front of the community centre, which was hidden behind a Londis, it was almost 10 p.m. He was nearly 90 minutes late. A well-built but not very tall forty-something with receding hair was walking around his battered, filthy, green Toyota Corolla, and smoking. When Damian got out of his shining A3, the man smiled and introduced himself. Damian wasn't sure, though, if the smile meant that Rob was happy to see him, or if it was rather an expression of how pathetic he thought Damian was. But the following day Rob called Damian and gave him the job, so it must have been the former.

***

A few days later, when Damian was waiting for a haircut at the barber's, leafing through The Irish Independent, he came across an ad for a journalist. Being interested in journalism, and having some experience in publishing, which he had gained while putting out a music magazine in his early years at university, he decided to chance his arm.

A man whose name was Tim emailed Damian in response to his application, but due to the lack of relevant experience, he couldn't consider Damian for the job. He thought, however, that Damian might be interested in another opportunity – that of a contributor to the weekly Polish-language supplement published with his paper. He suggested discussing it over coffee in O'Briens in Parnell Street the following week.

Still in the aftermath of his disastrously late arrival for the previous interview, Damian promised to himself that this time he would visit the place the day before in order to ensure he knew exactly where to meet Tim. But in the end he didn't.

On the day of the meeting, Damian got to Parnell Street at 9.55 a.m. – five minutes before the arranged time. He rushed all the way from the junction on Gardiner Street down Parnell Street to Capel Street looking for O'Briens, but there was no sign of it. He thought that blinded by the hurry he must have missed the café, so he went all the way back up. But again he couldn't find it. To make the situation even worse, he didn't have Tim's mobile number, nor had he noted down Tim's office number. And the local shopkeeper that Damian asked for directions, as much as she wanted to help, wasn't able to recall where O'Briens was. Damian had no other alternative but to walk down the long street once again. Halfway through, though, angry as hell, he stopped at the Centra beside the Jurys Inn Hotel to again ask for directions. But alas! The guy at the till said there was no O'Briens in Parnell Street that he knew of. Damian had had enough. Already over 20 minutes late, he felt it was high time he rang Tim's desk.

But first he needed to buy the paper from which he could get the editor's number. He found it quickly, dialled the number and then asked to be put through. Before he reached Tim's desk, though, his credit had run out. And now he was fuming! He ran back to the till – mad as a bull – got some credit, dialled the number again, and again asked to be put through to Tim.

"Hello, Tim's speaking!"

"Hello Tim! It's Damian. I was supposed to meet you half an hour ago, but..."

"Oh shit! Ah, that's right!" Tim interrupted. "Err... I completely forgot about it, Damian!"

"That's..." Damian hesitated for a second, "that's OK, Tim. Actually..."

"Listen!" Tim interrupted again. "I'm in the middle of something now, but would you be free to come up here in an hour or so?"

"Eh... I have to be somewhere else then, but I could come after lunch, if that's OK."

"Great! Pop into my office around two then."

The office happened to be only a stone's throw away from where Damian was standing. And he just couldn't believe his luck once again.

***

Damian now started getting hungry, so he ran across the street to the Kingfisher Restaurant for some grub. He wanted to have proper breakfast before his next meeting, which he hadn't lied to Tim about, and which was in the local Citizens Information Centre in O'Connell Street.

Someone with Polish-English translation and interpreting skills, as well as some basic knowledge of the law, was needed there to volunteer for a few hours a week, helping Polish people with whatever problems they might happen to stumble upon. Damian didn't have much knowledge of the law – or legal English, for that matter – but he was willing to learn.

Debby, an Irish lady who interviewed him in the centre, was very nice, though she seemed quite demanding. She offered him the position, but it required a few training sessions. They were to take place the following month, and they were to be attended by Damian and one other volunteer.

Damian readily accepted the position, but by the time the training was about to commence, he had become so busy with his other new job that he didn't even have enough time, nor energy, to answer Debby's emails, let alone go to the training. But one day she rang him to inform him that he had missed the training, and to enquire if he was still interested in working at the centre. He said he was, but he had to admit that he was now too busy to find enough free time to work as a volunteer.

Debby sounded disappointed, and Damian knew she had every right to be so. He felt embarrassed and unsure about why he had kept her in limbo for such a long time instead of just cancelling the whole thing.

But he was indeed very busy. Not that much with the paper, since it was mainly his girlfriend who wrote the articles (she had worked for a Polish radio station and a newspaper before she moved to Dublin, so she was equally – if not more – capable of writing quality stuff as Damian was; he would help her, though, if needed, do a bit of research, maybe change a few words here and there, and then he would email Tim the piece with his own name as the author; the money would be shared), but with the summer language school that he was now in charge of.

***

As soon as the job in Blanchardstown had occurred to be a mere cover for some other teacher, and Damian's working relationship with Rob, and Rob's business partner, a bit on the tense side of things, Damian applied for a job opening with a summer school to teach English to teenagers who are every July and August sent to Ireland in their thousands to practise the language.

When he was offered the gig, he happily accepted it, for – notwithstanding the regular pay cheques – sitting behind the rent-a-car counter and reading a paper for hours on end had long before proved too much of a bore.

But then, two days prior to Damian's start in the teaching job, he was offered a position of director of studies with the same school – a position that had suddenly become available. As much as it took him aback, Damian went for it without hesitation. He was sure it would be challenging, and he knew he was too young and too inexperienced for responsibilities of that sort, but all those anticipated difficulties simply made the job more appealing to him.

On his first day off, though, he slept like a child and couldn't wake up. He was totally exhausted. The workload was enormous, the psychological pressure unrelenting, and even physically the job was very demanding. He realised he had bitten off more than he could possibly chew.

But he somehow survived the summer, and – surprisingly enough – he even managed to impress the school's top director.

***

Damian stayed with the school for another year. But when the next summer passed and the place became quiet again, he started researching for his PhD. He felt it was the right time to go back to university.

One day, however, he came across an ad for a job that seemed to be cut out for him: a position for a linguist and translator.

As soon as Damian sent in his application, he received a phone call from an HR lady who was looking after that particular job opening. She was Polish, too, and she explained that the job was with Google in their European headquarters down in the docks. She said his CV looked really well, but she wanted to recommend a few changes so as to make it meet Google standards and thus increase Damian's chances of success.

Damian appreciated all the help, but as the job happened to be full-time – not part-time or flexi-time as he had been hoping, having in mind his PhD studies – he didn't worry too much about the whole thing. He did decide to pursue the job, though, if only to challenge himself and to see how far he could get in the recruitment process.

As suggested by the HR lady, Damian supplemented his CV with all his major successes, including the ones that seemed to him rather irrelevant – like, for instance, the successes he had achieved in competitive swimming when he was a teenager. Some detailed information about the hobbies and interests that he was actively involved in was also included. All those things, the HR lady said, mattered enormously to Google people.

And they indeed must have cared about them, because the next day Damian received a call from the same HR lady, saying that his CV had been accepted, and that he would shortly receive a phone screening. Before she hung up, she had advised Damian to make sure to research the main Google products – if he wasn't familiar with them – and to have a good understanding of how Google made their billions.

Damian followed her instructions to the letter, and when another HR specialist called to interview him – an Irish lady this time around – she said she was really impressed with his knowledge of the area, and that she was happy to schedule an hour-long, online-based test for him – a test that would assess Damian's practical knowledge of Google products, as well as his IT literacy. The test was to take place the following week, giving Damian a few additional days for research and preparation.

Damian used that time wisely, but when the day and the hour arrived, he didn't receive the link to the test. He waited anxiously for a while, but then he emailed the Polish HR lady and let her know that something must have gone wrong. He then logged into his other email account and was surprised to find the link there.

He quickly realised that the reason the link had been sent inappropriately must have been that the recruiters also had his old contact details on the system – most probably from the CV which he had left with them right after his arrival in Dublin. The Irish HR lady must have accidentally retrieved those old details when she wanted to send him the test.

Damian, however, even though he did find the link in his other account, and even though he did click on it to carefully explore the contents of the test, didn't mention anything to the Polish HR lady. And she didn't seem to have found out what had happened either, for when she called Damian later that day, she just apologised and explained that her colleague – the one responsible for sending the link – must have done something wrong. She also rescheduled the test for the following day.

Damian spent the rest of the day preparing the answers to the questions that he had seen under the link. He hoped the test the following day would be the same, or at least similar.

It was the same. The only thing Damian had to do was to make sure to accurately copy and paste all the answers he had prepared, and to load them before the allotted time was up – but not too early either, so as not to invite any suspicion.

Two days later, Damian received a call with warm congratulations on passing the test and an invitation to an on-site interview with the three managers of the team that he would be working with if he got offered the job. There would be three separate interviews, each with a different manager, and each with a different focus. Some questions, however, could well be repeated by the different managers, so he was advised to be consistent in his answers. He was also once again encouraged to refresh his knowledge of the main Google products, the company's background, as well as its main competitors.

***

Damian's interview was first thing in the morning on November 13. On arrival, he was collected from the reception by a young, chubby, knock-kneed Irish girl, whose name was Maggie, and who he thought was a secretary, even though he had read that as a rule there were no secretaries in Google. But he must have forgotten.

Maggie took Damian to the seventh floor, to a small meeting room with a glass wall overlooking the bay. It was cloudless outside, and the sea, the port and the Poolbeg chimneys looked absolutely stunning in the bright rays of the morning sun. She left him there for two minutes to help him make himself comfortable, and when she came back, she threw several questions and mini-tasks at him, most of which related to linguistics, and some of which didn't make much sense to Damian. He didn't hesitate to share those feelings with Maggie, and she seemed to appreciate that.

Then, there was Bernie – a baldish, thirty-something French guy with a strong accent. He had prepared a few mathematical and logical tasks. The main equation that he wanted to see solved could have been worked out in head, but Bernie insisted on having it presented step by step on the whiteboard hanging on the wall behind Damian. Being used to boards and markers, Damian enjoyed his presentation.

The last interview, and one that occurred to be the most chilled-out, was with Joaquin – a short but handsome Spanish lad with shoulder-length jet-black hair, who couldn't be much older than Damian. He was the team's main supervisor, which meant looking after everyone in the team, making sure that everyone there was happy, giving appraisals (one every two weeks), dealing with holiday requests, and generally being at hand in case any issue came up. They had a fairly casual chat, which made Damian quite open and honest about the fact that he indeed was interested in the job, but that he was rather busy with some other things. Joaquin listened attentively and was very inquisitive about Damian's plans for the future.

Before they parted, Joaquin promised Damian that he would be informed about their decision in less than a week.

***

On his way back home, Damian walked down Barrow Street towards Ringsend Road, and then left across the bridge over Grand Canal Dock. He walked slowly, making the most out of the warm, mid-November sunshine, and reflecting on the interview.

He continued his way towards the Liffey, past the Grand Canal Theatre, and then along the river in the direction of O'Connell Bridge. When he passed Sean O'Casey Bridge, his phone rang. It was Nigel from the HR department at Google. He wanted to congratulate Damian on impressing the team of managers and getting the job.

That unexpectedly swift decision took Damian by surprise, so much that apart from politely thanking Nigel he didn't know what to say when asked if he would accept the offer and be able to start at the beginning of December.

To buy some time, Damian told Nigel that he would first need to talk to his boss in the language school to see how much notice was required of him. He promised to call him back before the end of the day.

Damian of course didn't need to contact his boss. He knew the company rules perfectly well. What he needed was some extra time to weigh the pros and cons of accepting the offer. He had huge doubts about committing himself to another nine-to-five job, especially now – when he had finally managed to get round to researching some ideas for his doctoral thesis. He had been hoping that after the interview with the managers he would have some time to contemplate, free of any pressure, what would be the best thing for him to do.

It took Damian a few hours to mull it over, but he rang Nigel before the end of the day as promised. Before he could say *yes*, though, he requested that his starting date be postponed to January. He explained he would need that extra time to finish the projects that he was involved in. It was all true, but he also secretly hoped the company might not be able to accommodate him, which, in turn, would nicely make the problem of deciding about what to do solve itself.

But Nigel checked the thing in no time and there was no problem. Damian was expected to start work right after the Christmas break. The contract was to be posted to him within days.

***

The decision to start work at Google created a sense of unease that Damian could do without in his life. And his anxiety was growing as the time was passing. He hated doing things that he wasn't totally sure of.

The good news was, however, that although it was now already well into December, his contract still hadn't arrived. It gave Damian a glimmer of hope that he had been forgotten about. And by no means was he eager to remind anyone.

When flying away for Christmas, still without a contract in his mail box, Damian had already decided that he wouldn't be clocking in on January 4 – the date suggested by the recruiter. Over Christmas, his family was supportive, yet they were also trying to persuade him that the job might actually be worth going for, because, after all, it was with Google. But Damian had already made up his mind.

After Christmas, he and his girlfriend went to Scotland for a few days to visit Edinburgh and Glasgow.

They got back to Dublin on the night of January 3. Still in bed the next morning, Damian heard his mobile vibrate, but being half asleep, he didn't bother to check who it was. The phone kept ringing, though, and it made him think that something must have been wrong – and in an instant he realised that it was the very morning that he was supposed to collect his Google badge.

Damian's eyes opened big as ping-pong balls. And at that same moment he received a voice mail. But as he wasn't sure what he would say, he looked for an excuse not to check it. And he was right: it was Nigel wondering where he was and saying that the team were waiting for him in the office on Barrow Street.

Still in bed, Damian started experiencing self-doubt and serious pricks of conscience. He suddenly understood that the whole thing should have been dealt with in a different, perhaps more civilised manner. His phone rang again, but again he didn't answer.

He got up, and while picking some food from the fridge, he heard his phone ring once again. This time he didn't even check who was calling. He put on the kettle. But while preparing and then having breakfast, he grew increasingly uneasy about the whole situation, realising that he would eventually need to answer the phone.

The terrible butterflies that he had didn't let him eat much. He took his coffee to bed, and there, under the duvet, he kept criticising himself for how irresponsible he was. At the same time, though, his vanity had been flattered. He felt important to those people who were there waiting for him with high hopes. He felt he owed them something, and thought it might actually not be the worst idea in the world to give the Google gig a try. But how would he explain his absence on the first day?

***

Damian contemplated lying about a missed flight to Dublin, but then he realised they might in that situation expect him to come to the office the following day, or as soon as possible, and he didn't feel like doing that. He had already agreed to prepare some course materials for the school, and so he would be glued to the blue screen for at least a couple of weeks.

Trying to collect his thoughts for another hour or so, Damian eventually made up his mind: he would work for Google, and he would lie about missing his first day.

He got out of bed, went to the living room, and stood by the window the way he usually stood when making a call about something important – resting his elbows on the window sill and looking out onto the street. It was a freezing day, and it had just started snowing.

"Hi Nigel," Damian put on a solemn and hushed tone of voice. "Sorry for missing your calls earlier today, but I'm in hospital and I only got the chance to ring you now."

"What happened?! Are you OK?!" Nigel sounded genuinely worried.

"My dad had a heart attack last Saturday, and we're here today sorting things out with the doctors."

"Oh… I'm really sorry to hear that, Damian. How is he now?"

"He's fine. Thanks. Everything seems to be under control now, and the doctors are optimistic. They say he's recovering really fast. He had some important checks done this morning. And we've just been talking to the doctors trying to get our heads around it."

Damian felt it was all wrong, but he kept going, "I'm sorry, Nigel. I know I should have let you know earlier. But I just wasn't thinking straight."

Damian's father had indeed had a heart attack, a few years before, so the whole excuse, Damian thought, was partially true, and that made him feel slightly less disgusted with himself. He then lied to Nigel that he wanted to stay by his dad's bed for another two or three weeks.

A month later, Damian sat in that spacious, shining lobby of the European headquarters of the biggest search engine in the world, opposite a long reception desk, patiently waiting for Joaquin to collect him and introduce him to his colleagues. This time, Damian had ensured he wouldn't arrive late.

CPSIA information can be obtained at www.ICGtesting.com
Printed in the USA
LVOW12s1914080914

403037LV00006B/720/P

9 780992 813215

THE NEW DUBLINERS